**W9-BFR-600**

"The expectations of this workforce combined with the millennial generation will force the workplace to change. This book gives a leader insights into what makes that new evolved worker tick, and how the change in the marketplace has to occur to unleash this global talent. To figure out how to leverage this talent will be the competitive advantage for any business as our historic 'contract' with employees is no longer valid. A must read."

—Pat Wadors, VP, Global Talent Organization, LinkedIn

"For anyone engaged in the Innovation Economy, or hoping to better understand today's mobile, agile workforce, *The Rise of the Naked Economy* is an insightful, interesting and enjoyable read. Ryan Coonerty and Jeremy Neuner translate their insights and experience in the working world to the printed page without missing a beat. I highly recommend it."

—Carl Guardino, President and CEO,
Silicon Valley Leadership Group

"Coonerty and Neuner's examination of the radical shift in the relationship between employer and employee in the new economy is a must read for anyone entering the workforce, and perhaps even more important for those of us who have been here for years. A timely and fascinating book."

—Len Vlahos, Executive Director,
Book Industry Study Group

"Workplaces in corporate America are beginning to embrace a whole new way of working that has been pioneered by entrepreneurial individuals. *The Rise of the Naked Economy* provides the understanding you need to lead your organization or to enter the emerging society of individual entrepreneurs."

—Ken Kannappan, CEO of Plantronics

"*The Rise of the Naked Economy* has struck a chord. Ryan Coonerty and Jeremy Neuner have encapsulated the changes facing employees and their employers in today's marketplace. It is insightful, humorous, filled with stories and opportunities for instant application. I think it nothing less than revolutionary in how they approach and describe the changes facing our economy."

—Gayle Shanks, co-owner of Changing Hands Bookstore

"A fascinating look at the workplace revolution, *The Rise of the Naked Economy* is filled with compelling stories about people creating and pursuing work in innovative ways. Coonerty and Neuner aren't just thinking outside the box, they're imaging a world without boxes. And after reading their book, you'll be as excited as they clearly are about this brave new world."

—Allison Hill, President/COO, Vroman's Bookstore

PREVIOUS BOOKS BY RYAN COONERTY

Etched in Stone: Enduring Words from Our National Monuments (National Geographic, 2007)

THE RISE
OF THE
NAKED
ECONOMY

HOW TO BENEFIT FROM THE
CHANGING WORKPLACE

RYAN COONERTY AND JEREMY NEUNER

palgrave
macmillan

First published in 2013 by PALGRAVE MACMILLAN® in the United
States—a division of St. Martin's Press LLC, 175 Fifth Avenue, New York,
NY 10010.

Where this book is distributed in the UK, Europe and the rest of
the world, this is by Palgrave Macmillan, a division of Macmillan
Publishers Limited, registered in England, company number 785998,
of Houndmills, Basingstoke, Hampshire
RG21 6XS.

Palgrave Macmillan is the global academic imprint of the above
companies and has companies and representatives throughout the
world.

Palgrave® and Macmillan® are registered trademarks in the United
States, the United Kingdom, Europe and other countries.

ISBN 978-0-230-34219-4

Library of Congress Cataloging-in-Publication Data

Coonerty, Ryan.
   The rise of the naked economy : how to benefit from the changing
workplace / Ryan Coonerty and Jeremy Neuner.
      pages   cm
   Includes index.
   ISBN 978-0-230-34219-4 (alk. paper)
   1. Work—Social aspects. 2. Success in business. I. Neuner, Jeremy.
II. Title.
HD6955.C665   2013
650.1—dc23

                                                        2012048230

A catalogue record of the book is available from the British Library.

Design by Letra Libre, Inc.

First edition: July 2013

10 9 8 7 6 5 4 3 2 1

Printed in the United States of America.

For Emily and Becca

CONTENTS

FOREWORD

A ONCE-IN-A-CENTURY OPPORTUNITY

Fueled by technology and changing lifestyles, work is undergoing a transformation not seen since the Industrial Revolution. Just a generation ago, typical employees could land a job with a large company right out of college and reasonably expect to stay there for their entire career. Contrast that with this startling fact from the US Bureau of Labor Statistics: as of 2010, the average time an American worker stays at any job had plummeted to less than four and a half years.

Now fast-forward to our not-so-distant future. It's a brave new world where half of all workers are self-employed "fractional workers," that is, they work with multiple clients on a variety of jobs. Telecommuting has now replaced the daily 9-to-5 grind, and fractional hiring is as commonplace as full-time employment. For an ever-growing group of workers, that future is here. Meet 36-year-old Alexandra: In a typical month she works with five different employers, bids on seven new jobs, is a member of two virtual teams, and attends many virtual meetings, including a few in the middle of the night for a client in

Stockholm and another in Tel Aviv. She describes herself simply as a twenty-first-century worker. To the rest of us Alexandra stands as an iconic example of the new workforce.

None of this would have been possible—or even imaginable—just a few short years ago. The self-employed once relied on business cards and handshakes at networking events, often leaving flyers at local shops and mailing postcards to nearby businesses. Their reach was limited to how far they could drive in a day. Work was inconsistent at best, and getting paid was a constant nightmare. The risk of leaving steady employment kept all but the most fearless workers from striking out on their own.

To say the least, things have changed immensely. Today the opportunities for fractional work are exploding, as is the development of tools that allow people to work independently. A freelancer today can monitor job demand online, connect with businesses anywhere with a few keystrokes, and completely automate payment collection through platforms like Elance. Shared workspace can be accessed through coworking companies like NextSpace, and new skills can be learned on platforms like Lynda.com. It is an exciting time for those hiring and for those ready to adopt a new way of working, and the future only looks bright.

A quick look at industry statistics validates the tremendous employment opportunities and earning potential for fractional workers. Many larger companies report that 30 percent of their procurement dollars are spent on contingent and fractional workers. Similarly, an estimated 30 percent of those in today's job market—or roughly 42 million workers—are either self-employed or part time. Conservative estimates put this number at more than 40 percent by the end of the decade.

Elance is seeing an even sharper growth curve. As the world's most popular online staffing service, Elance has seen freelancers earn $700 million. Annual earnings on Elance are approaching $300 million. To grasp how large this market is, Elance today has more than two million registered freelancers in 155 countries working for 250,000 active clients on every continent. Businesses of all sizes are posting one million jobs annually and are receiving nine million candidates from Elance. And we see much more growth ahead: more than 25,000 new freelancers and 7,500 new businesses are signing up each week. Pretty amazing figures.

However, the quickly emerging twenty-first-century worker also faces new challenges. Because work can be done anywhere, global competition is everywhere. No longer does one region have a leg up on talent and skills. Similarly, workers who market themselves effectively are finding plenty of work, while equally good workers with a less dominant marketing gene can't find enough. Also the lack of health insurance is a huge problem for many, as the decline in full-time employment brings with it the loss of many benefits people have come to expect from our employer-based health insurance system.

The Rise of the Naked Economy is about all aspects of this transformation of work and the emerging new workforce. Brimming with humor and insights, the book explores what makes the twenty-first-century worker tick. If you believe yesterday's way of matching available jobs with qualified talent is riddled with inefficiencies, or if you're a manager, marketer, educator, or a parent with a child destined for the workforce, this book will make you smarter and more prepared for the inevitable changes. It will make you take a good hard look at the most profound transformation in our workforce in the last 100 years.

I thank the authors for beginning this important dialogue. This book allows all of us—from workers to employers to government policy makers—to begin discussing these enormous, once-in-a-century changes in our workforce, our economy, and our society. More important, this book provides insights on how to smooth the transition. Throughout the book the authors introduce you to a range of brave, talented people like Alexandra who are at the forefront of this shift. Make no mistake: they are writing about true pioneers, those who work differently today and are the future of work tomorrow.

Fabio Rosati, CEO, Elance
Mountain View, California
October 2012

INTRODUCTION

THE NAKED ECONOMY

Being naked approaches being revolutionary; going bare-foot is mere populism.

—John Updike

Are you ready for the naked economy?

In May 2010, four coworkers in London rode naked on the Tube during their morning commute. Wearing nothing but shoes, the coed quartet made quite an impression on more stodgily dressed commuters. While we might dismiss this stunt as mere exhibitionism, these workers had a loftier goal in mind. By spending an entire workday together naked—from the morning commute through daily office routines to the evening wind-down over what we might guess was more than a few drinks—members of the group wanted to break down barriers, improve communication, and develop a higher level of trust among themselves.

In these tough economic times, people will try anything to improve productivity, get an edge on the competition, and find some release from the monotony of meetings, e-mails, and conference calls. Since then this experiment has been repeated dozens of times at offices and workplaces around the world. Warning: You might want to take close stock of yourself and your coworkers before considering trying it at your place of work.

You'll be pleased and relieved to know that, in our version of the Naked Economy, we can all keep our clothes on. *In fact, what we're suggesting in* The Rise of the Naked Economy *is much more radical than simply showing up at work in the buff.*

After all, is trudging through the same mundane tasks that fill your day without your clothes on really all that revolutionary? This is not about whether your rear end should be covered when it hits your office chair but whether it needs to be there at all. This is an essential question not just for you but for our economy. We believe that if we want to create jobs, increase our collective potential for innovation, and maybe even save the planet and our sanity, we need to completely rethink how we've organized our economy. And we need to start by stripping work bare.

Here's a list of a few things that need to go:

- Your 45-minute commute through snarled traffic to the office
- Your cubicle (heck, your entire office building could probably go, too)
- Managers who see their purpose as managing you rather than the project
- Your company-sponsored health insurance plan
- Your company-sponsored retirement plan
- Most of your coworkers and colleagues (don't worry, they're not gone forever; you'll bump into them again in all sorts of strange and wonderful places)

- The culture that says 2 P.M. on Mondays (no matter the weather, your children's schedule, or how you feel) belongs to your employer, while 2 P.M. on Saturdays is "your time"
- Two weeks for vacations, two weeks for sickness, and two months for the birth of your child
- Your job itself (it's not what you really wanted to do anyway)
- Your 45-minute commute through snarled traffic back home

Sound radical? Scary? And maybe just a bit refreshing? *The Rise of the Naked Economy* is all these . . . if you're looking at the economy with the eyes of an early twenty-first-century worker. As a species we've been going to work, in one form or another, for the better part of 100,000 years. Yet the trappings (and the traps) of modern work have been with us for less than 100 years—a mere blip in human history. This book is about stripping work down to its bare essence and rethinking our economy in a way that takes advantage of changes in technology and priorities, and of the unmatched power of simple face-to-face human interaction.

Work and the world are changing in fundamental ways. We'll meet people, companies, and policy makers who are driving that change and already living prosperously from it. More dramatically, this book tells how the rise of the Naked Economy will literally reorder our society—and, if done correctly—will allow people to rediscover and reclaim some of their fundamental humanity and live more productive, happier, and sustainable lives.

In Part I, "The Cubicle Pensioner: The Traps and Trappings of Work," we explore the rise and fall of the social contract between workers and their employers. The old contract, based on job security in exchange for loyalty, was nice while it lasted, but it left on the outside looking in huge parts of our population that needed flexibility—mainly women, the young, and older workers who have to balance competing priorities for their time. Not to mention billions of people around the world who were never offered the health benefits, safe working conditions, or a gold watch for their years of service. The new social contract will be based on a different mix of economic drivers, collaboration, and personal priorities.

In Part II, "A Specialist and Generalist Walk into a Bar . . . Get Drunk, and Start a Company," we analyze the skill sets and organizational structures that will thrive in the Naked Economy. Super Specialists, who can find their niche in a connected globalized economy and constantly hone their skills, will be able to set their price and schedules. Smart Generalists will need to pull talent together in project-based teams in ways that bridge gaps in culture, information, and technology. Finally, new organizational structures must be devised based on the recognition that the talent that innovative organizations need should not have to live within 50 miles of the office.

Finally, in Part III, "Wi-fi, Work, and Water Coolers—How Work Is Changing but People Are Not," we focus on the "three P's," which will provide the new infrastructure for a thriving economy: people, place, and policy. Interestingly, despite the remarkable technological advances since the early 1990s, the Naked Economy requires putting people first: understanding what makes them creative, innovative, and productive, not to mention happy. A large element in recruiting, retaining, and accessing these happy people is ending the arbitrary physical barriers that we constructed for the old economy. We will need new places to gather, work, live, and interact. These new spaces will be a small piece of the infrastructure for the new economy. Businesses, nonprofits, and policy makers will need to craft new strategies, just as they did for earlier economic revolutions in agriculture, industry, and information.

This book examines how work has morphed from a physical place to a kind of mind-set of shared goals and values, and how stripping away the hassles and restrictions of the old-style office makes its benefits all the more apparent. Because humans don't evolve as quickly as technology does, we'll explain why office Christmas parties still matter and why you (yes, *you*) need to get out of your skivvies (an ironic reality in the Naked Economy) and be with real live people.

Yet this emerging new economy cannot happen in a vacuum. Government and private-sector policies must be in place to allow the new paradigm to take hold for the benefit of both labor and capital. Cooperation is the key, or most of us will be left behind. So we'd better start asking the big questions now: What are the policies and platforms for the new economy? Do we have the foresight, patience, and guts to rewire our mindsets and our business, legal, and political systems? How do we ensure that everyone will have the opportunity to work and live prosperously in the Naked Economy? Will the new way to work allow us to turn off our phones and interact like normal human beings, or will future generations be a bunch of twitching weirdos as inane information is wired directly into their cerebral cortex?

This book is not meant to have all the answers. Nor are we the first to ask the questions. Authors Dan Pink and Richard Florida recognized this trend more than ten years ago and have done amazing work to reshape our national debate around fostering creativity and building an economy based on creative knowledge workers.[1] Sara Horowitz founded the Freelancers Union also a decade ago in response to the rapid rise of the freelance economy and the lack of a social structure to support that economy.[2] She won a MacArthur Foundation "genius grant" for her efforts. If you think that the new economy needs to be more just and stable than the last one, pay attention and support her movement.

As cofounders of more than a half-dozen coworking spaces with over 1,000 members—all of whom personify the free-agent–creative-class professionals imagined by Pink and Florida and who face the challenges that Horowitz aims to solve—we are attempting to pick up where Pink, Florida, and Horowitz left off, providing a view from the front lines of this revolution where the new infrastructure and culture of work are being imagined and put into practice with amazing success.

The economic transition of the first decade of the twenty-first century was not easy. Tens of millions of workers were displaced, and economic insecurity caused stress and profound cultural turmoil. These workers may see the Naked Economy as just one more step toward leaving them and their family literally naked against the blizzards of a globalized economy. But it needn't be that way. The rise of the Naked Economy, like all revolutions, will not be smooth, and not everyone will benefit. However, with awareness of the economic, cultural, and demographic trends that are causing this shift and some smart strategies, we have a chance to build a better world. If you care about the future competitiveness of our economy; the daily well-being of you, your family, and community; and the health of our planet, read on—clothing is optional.

PART 1

THE CUBICLE PENSIONER

The Traps and Trappings of Work

CHAPTER 1

WE ARE ALL SELF-EMPLOYED

"Free Your Mind . . . And Your Ass Will Follow."
—Funkadelic album title

THE NOTEBOOK

At 33, Shane Pearlman has surfed some of the best breaks in the world, authored a nationally recognized city policy, finished a couple of triathlons, and started a company and a family.[1] But his Dreams List, as he calls it, won't let him rest.

He still has to get within 20 feet of an orca in the wild and surf the Amazon tidal bore (ideally not at the same time).

He still has to have lunch with a billionaire and get a Christmas card from the White House.

He still has to dance at his daughter's wedding, teach his grandkids how to fly a kite, and court his wife until the day he dies.

It's a lot to do, but every day he wakes up and gets a little more of it done. To keep track and stay on schedule, he writes these and hundreds of other goals down in a square black notebook. It's the first thing this entrepreneur reaches for whenever he needs to decide how to schedule his time. Inside that note-book is a running checklist that he's kept for a decade, of goals, dreams, and plans, grand and mundane, personal and professional.

This notebook not only is how he guides his days and nights but also will be how he determines, when he is sitting on his porch surrounded by grandkids half a century from now, whether he lived a life worth living.

The notebook was born during Shane's "quarter-life cri-sis," when, just out of college, he was laid off five times in two years. Struggling to make sense of a work world for which he had prepared but that didn't seem to want him, Shane turned to a mentor, who suggested he change his perspective—away from the kind of job he needed and toward the kind of life he wanted. It was then that he purchased the notebook, for put-ting his aspirations down on paper, and his days shifted from chasing elusive job security to finding fulfillment.

Now he returns to the notebook every month or so to check off his accomplishments, add more goals, and erase what is no longer relevant. As he explains, "I think the deep-est value of the Dreams List is that it is a road map. Not so much to judge success in the past but provide a series of des-tinations that allows you to make more intentional choices at the many crossroads that life offers." Four times a year his company holds a retreat during which he urges his partners to judge their success by their own notebooks. This kind of rigorous introspection and peer accountability is what Shane believes gives meaning to his day, makes him driven and fo-cused and, most of all, happy.

He did not win the lottery, he hasn't got a trust fund, and his company has not gone public. He is a middle-class family man with the responsibilities many of us have—a mortgage, child care, and a spouse who was laid off and is looking for a new career. He has to work just like the rest of us.

Yet because he made having a good life a priority, he went from being chronically laid off to a thriving career niche running a technical talent agency that works with other freelancers for local start-ups and Fortune 500 companies. The work is designed to conform to his life, or, as he puts it, "I plan my life, then my work. That's why I call it a lifestyle business," which he defines as "enough money to have choices and enough time to do the things that make life worth living."

THE GAME HAS CHANGED

Such a life seemed just as impossible to him a few years ago as it may feel to many of us today, when the rules of work are 9 to 5, Monday to Friday, with a couple of weeks of vacation a year and the near-constant requirement to be available by phone, instant messaging, or e-mail. At the time, Shane was following the model of what it means to "go to work" that we collectively have followed for a couple of generations. The model worked for a lot of people, including both of Shane's parents, who worked nearly their entire lives as engineers for one company. He expected to take a similar path and, like millions of his contemporaries, have a similar outcome—the stable job, nice house, and 2.5 kids who then work hard and do better than their parents.

"I went to college. I got the A's that I was supposed to get. I got the degree. I had the family that could guide me, support me, mentor me, that had the connections," he said. "I really had all the right cards."

He may have had the right cards, but the game had changed. In 1999, when he first entered the workforce, Shane, an anthropology major who had taught himself how to write computer code, chose the notoriously volatile Silicon Valley dot-com industry to begin his career. In "the Valley," an employee's experience was much more gold rush than gold watch: the postwar model of catching on with a paternalistic blue-chip firm, putting in your 30 years, and retiring to take up fly-fishing on a generous pension was already disappearing.

Today, companies in all sectors of the post-globalization world economy are taking their cues from the Silicon Valley way of work, which has been aptly described by the New York University sociologist Dalton Conley as "work constantly, live uneasily."[2] As a result we are quickly changing from a world of payroll employees to a world of independent free agents.

Shane learned this the hard way. He bounced from jobs in education to high tech. In every position he worked hard and was committed, but after five successive layoffs it became apparent to him that he was trading his freedom—the ability to live a life that included surfing in the middle of the day or just hanging out with his wife—for the illusory security of a "real job." If the game had changed, it was time to make a new set of rules, but this time on his terms.

"EVERYONE IS AN ENTREPRENEUR"

The rules of work have changed. Fundamental leaps in technology, demographics, and economics are driving a once-a-century shift in how, when, where, and why we work. The traditional way of making a living is not only increasingly untenable but undesirable. The whens and wheres of the new workplace still matter, but increasingly the bigger questions are the hows and the whys.

Workers are almost always the first victims of seismic economic upheavals, but people like Shane will tell you that they don't have to be. For those workers who want to clock their 40 hours for "the Man" and devote their free time to watching ESPN and adorable cat videos on YouTube, letting someone else worry about China and Wall Street, the news is not good. In the age of globalization, companies are under intense pressure to find more and more efficiencies in the way they do business. Using new platforms, they will be able to find people for specific tasks on demand and do it far more easily and inexpensively than hiring just the right person for a career.

Consider the observation by the Princeton economist Alan Blinder that almost 30 percent of the jobs in the United States, including lawyers, accountants, and other traditional "good jobs," can be outsourced.[3] Even those jobs that aren't outsourced will be done differently. Companies like LiveOpps, Elance, TaskRabbit, and Mechanical Turk are investing hundreds of millions in building platforms that aggregate human talent globally on a task-by-task basis. LiveOpps, a company of 300 employees, contracts with more than 20,000 people to run virtual call centers out of people's homes and on their schedules. Those numbers pale in comparison to Amazon's Mechanical Turk, which uses more than 100,000 workers from 100 countries to perform specific tasks for an average of $1.40 an hour.

Successful workers in the new century are those who will adopt an entrepreneurial mind-set, because essentially that's what they'll have to be. Entrepreneur is a term that is gradually losing its elitist mystique, which is a good thing. The self-employment guru Chris Guillebeau, author of *The $100 Startup,* used to live in Sierra Leone, where he learned a thing or two at the village marketplaces.[4] "In West Africa, everybody's an entrepreneur," he said.[5]

Luckily, there has never been a better time in history to be an entrepreneur. The barriers to starting a new business have dramatically fallen away, and in many cases the capital outlay and risk are minimal. Just ask teenager Maddie Bradshaw of Dallas, who started a multimillion-dollar business selling designer bottle cap magnets in 2006 from her kitchen table and still found time to be on the school's swim team.[6] Or YouTube "stars" who are pulling down six figures performing in their living rooms and virtual CEOs running companies from their boats in the Bahamas. As the myth of job security with a big company begins to fade, the American Dream will again recalibrate to something similar to what it originally was—the dream of being in charge of your own destiny.

LIVE, WORK—IN THAT ORDER

The vanguard of workers is taking a different approach to work and life. The stark demarcations between work time and leisure time, between professional life and private life, will soon become as antique as three-piece suits and fax machines. Instead workers will integrate their participation in the economy with their desire for a good life, leading to more introspection about the meaning of work and demand that it serve a higher purpose.

This is at the center of Shane Pearlman's life and business strategy. Over time he has gone from a freelance web developer to running a small army of website coders, designers, and developers with his partner, Peter Chester. To keep the company true to their ideals, they periodically take a step back from day-to-day business in order to refocus on the long view using what they call the "Six F's": family, friends, finance, fitness, faith, and fun. The hours he and Peter spend surfing, training for triathlons, and tending to their young families are not, in their view, parts of a private life they keep in a separate Tupperware container from their work life. They are means of fulfillment and self-improvement that lead directly to a more productive business life and vice versa.

Recent studies have demonstrated that creativity and effectiveness in the workplace require more, not less, time off and that sitting at a desk will literally take years off your life.[7] If Shane and Peter's team thinks that any of the "Six F's" are out of whack, they will turn down work, give team members more time off, and generally try to bring their lives back into balance. This keeps everyone happy, productive, and profitable.

For older generations of workers, finding a job was everything. For people today finding a direction is increasingly more important. So what are the implications of having a workforce determined to be something other than cogs in the corporate machine?

For the traditional workplace the implications are profound. For generations "the office" has been the central focus of work life, as well as the primary place for encountering the world outside the home—why do you think so many television comedies and dramas are set in one version or another of *The Office?*

Technology has removed the primary justification for workers to be in one physical space at one set time. In that sense, the laptop, tablet, and smart phone have become genuine tools of liberation. According to the market research firm International Data Corporation, there will be more than 1.3 billion mobile workers—workers who can work anywhere—by 2015.[8] That is 37 percent of the global workforce. What happens to the gross national product when workers don't have to commute in carbon-spewing vehicles and sit in soul-crushing traffic, when companies don't have to invest in cubicle farms to warehouse bitter workers who could easily do their jobs from their kitchen tables or neighborhood parks? What happens to family life when Mom and Dad don't have to set schedules with military precision to get to work, soccer games, dance recitals, and the occasional rushed family dinner?

Millions of workers are already fashioning more favorable schedules for themselves in places of their own choosing. A 2012 survey commissioned by Wrike, a project management company, found that 83 percent of respondents reported working from home for at least part of their workday and 66 percent believed that their office could be completely virtual within the next five years.[9] The Naked Economic revolution has begun.

FRONTLINES OF THE REVOLUTION

We see the Naked Economy everyday in our business, NextSpace. NextSpace is a coworking company that (as of this writing) operates seven coworking spaces around California. What is coworking? The traditional office, for all its gross inefficiencies, still offers the valuable resource of face-to-face camaraderie. So a new industry began a few years ago to provide self-styled work spaces for freelancers, entrepreneurs, and other independent professionals—the Shane Pearlmans of the world—where they could engage with other humans on their own terms and schedule.

We stumbled on coworking in 2008, when we, as the mayor and economic development manager, respectively, for the City of Santa Cruz, California, were looking for a new way to do economic development and provide a place for the increasing number of talented citizens trying to find a way to stay employed and live in our coastal community. When we saw our coffee shops full of people with laptops working for companies and for themselves, we decided it was time to flip our economic model on its outdated head: instead of attracting one 200-person company to Santa Cruz, we would create a space for 200 one-person companies.

Jeremy quit his job, we wrote a business plan, raised money, and joined the coworking movement, opening our first NextSpace. Our spaces provide hip, comfortable, professional work spaces—desks, café tables, comfy couches, speedy Internet, shared printers, and all the tea, coffee, and other caffeine-delivery devices that you can consume—along with a professional collaborative community of people who are living, breathing, and succeeding in this new economy.

This focus on collaborative community is the driving force behind our business. NextSpace members don't need cubicles, corporate campuses, 401(k) plans, and the other golden handcuffs of the modern economy to be successful. But they do need each other.

Take the story of a scrappy little mobile application company called Fuel 4 Humans. NextSpace member Renata de LaRocque is a nutritionist who works independently to help people with diabetes make better choices about their diets.[10] Given the enormous rise of diabetes in the United States,

Renata knew she was serving a huge and growing market. To serve that market, grow her business, and, she hoped, make a better living, Renata needed a way to reach more clients. A friend told her that she should build an iPhone app that tells people with diabetes what they should buy in the grocery store. A great idea, Renata told herself. But she's a nutritionist and doesn't know the first thing about creating mobile apps.

So Renata found fellow NextSpace member Einar Vollset, a former computer science professor at Cornell University who left academia to hop on the mobile applications bandwagon as a freelance programmer. Einar doesn't know the first thing about nutrition or diabetes, but he can build iPhone apps in his sleep. When the app was finished, both Einar and Renata realized that it needed a logo and an icon before they could submit it to the Apple app store.

Of course neither knew a thing about graphic design. But NextSpace member Eric Ressler, the principal at a small graphic design studio called Cosmic, knew plenty about design and quickly ginned up an icon for the app. Pleased with her progress so far, Renata told herself, "Wow, Fuel 4 Humans could be bigger than I thought! I should probably start a new legal entity around Fuel 4 Humans so it can be a real company." So she found Ian Stock, a corporate attorney and NextSpace member. Ian was a partner in a few high-flying law firms in New York, Paris, and Silicon Valley but left the rat race to start a solo practice called Entreprelaw. Ian did the legal work for Renata quicker than you can say "limited liability." And, through the collective efforts of four very different people with four different but complementary skill sets, Fuel 4 Humans was born. They each used their skill sets, worked collaboratively in a place and in a manner that worked for their lives, and maintained their sanity and humanity in the process.

If that's not a recipe for innovation and job creation, we don't know what is. To us, the beauty of Fuel 4 Humans is that it was created in the early days of this economic shift and stands as an iconic example of what we think the Naked Economy should look like in the future. Instead of big, static organizations creating and delivering the value they tell us we need, small groups of individuals come together for a specific purpose that they believe in to give us what we want. And they do so on their terms, as part of a balanced life. When their job is done, they disband and reassemble in a new group around a new project. Repeat this process a million times over, and you have a good idea of the nature and prospects for success in the Naked Economy.

At NextSpace, we see this process happening over and over again, all day, every day, in large and small ways. In fact, our value (remember, most members can work for free in coffee shops or at home) is that we create an environment in which these interactions occur. We call it managed serendipity; others call it "community."

Our members represent an incredibly broad and deep ecosystem of all sorts of complementary skills: writers, programmers, software developers, entrepreneurs, designers, accountants, editors, attorneys, architects, marketing and public relations pros, filmmakers, and artists. We purposely do not limit our membership to specific industries or skills because we believe that a diverse community generates more opportunity and just plain interesting moments. Often, during NextSpace Happy Hours, at brown bag lunches, or over a cup of coffee (always caffeinated), our members simply share bits of expertise with each other, making each other just a bit smarter, more productive, and inspired. Sometimes they team up to tackle projects together. And in more than a few cases, as with Fuel 4 Humans, they're the driving force behind the creation of new products and new companies. But the pattern is always the same: the constant assembly, disassembly, and reassembly of people, talent, and ideas around a range of challenges and opportunities. NextSpace even boasts a sex therapist, an ordained minister, and a stand-up comic as members. Based on regularly watching projects like Fuel 4 Humans develop in NextSpace, and on listening to the dozens of people we interviewed for this book, we identified two key players in the Naked Economy: big-picture thinkers, who we call the Smart Generalists, and the small-bore experts, the Super Specialists.

Think back to the stories in this chapter and see how talent is deployed in a new way, leading to economic opportunity matched with personal values. The Smart Generalists, the Shane Pearlmans of the world, people whose experience is wide rather than deep, will find the world has a consistent demand for those who can manage, synthesize, troubleshoot, and problem solve. At the same time the Super Specialists—the Renata de LaRocques, Ian Stocks, and Einar Vollsets—will be a valuable asset in the most important aspect of business success in the new economy: finding a creative and lucrative niche in the global talent market. All designed their work to match their life's needs and values.

Even in a world of free agents working in their own style and time, the company, (albeit in a much different form) is still the prime organizing principle of the economy. Humans have always come together for common purpose—trade guilds,

quilting bees, flash mobs, conferences, orgies, coworking communities, and social networking. Those companies that are
adapting to the new world by allowing their workers the freedom to dictate their own work styles will find happier workers,
bigger profits, and more prosperity.

Shane is a living example of what the future of work might
look like. He purposefully uses the term "evangelist" to describe
himself and in that word is an inherent promise: If he, Renata,
and Einar can shape their work lives to their preferences and
desires, then so can the rest of us. So let's go . . .

CHAPTER 2

FROM HUNTER-GATHERERS TO TPS REPORTS

A (Mixed) History of Work

The future ain't what it used to be.

—Yogi Berra

WORK LIKE A CAVEMAN

In the beginning there was work.

Work is, and has always been, a nonnegotiable condition of survival. From the moment the first hominids scampered across the African savannas, the human species has been consumed by the work of staying alive. Our oldest ancestors are often referred to as hunter-gatherers, because that was their work. They hunted, they gathered, they protected what they had hunted and gathered, every hour of every day until they found themselves on the business end of a hyena. In fact, some studies show that hunter-gathers worked only three hours a day, then basically hung out for the rest of the day.[1] Once again proving that evolution isn't all it's cracked up to be.

Is our daily working life all that different from that of the hunter-gatherers? Sure, advances in technology, science, art, and coffee have been amazing. But unless you count loincloths and shaving habits, not a lot has changed. We wake up and start hunting and gathering—new leads, sales, connections, stocks that will go up, or prices that will go down. We have traded a spear for a smart phone and the wide-open plains for a cubicle, but the purpose of work remains the same.

The single most salient difference between early humans and contemporary humans is not why but how—and, more strikingly, how quickly—the nature of work has changed.

Early humans were engaged in the basic subsistence of hunting and gathering for *two million* years; during that period cultural evolution took hundreds of generations and technological advances took a millennium. Today we witness fundamental, even radical, social and economic change within a decade. This rate of change has made us more adaptable than the generations before us. But when it comes to work, an activity as central to human life as eating, sleeping, and procreating—though not nearly as enjoyable—we don't have the opportunity to analyze and control what is happening to our lives. We are happy if we just keep our dental plan.

In fact, we seem to be largely oblivious to the changes taking place in our midst. Few of us seem to be mindful of what's happening to the nature of work, even in the teeth of a period of economic upheaval.

The complex nexus of settings, behaviors, relationships, and arrangements that we recognize today as work—cubicles, time cards, paychecks, hierarchical levels of management, casual Fridays, Super Bowl betting pools—is a relatively recent development, however much we think of it as inevitable as the sun coming up in the morning. Remember, if the whole of human history were compressed into the life of one 40-year-old worker, the creation of the modern workplace happened the day before yesterday.

BLAME THE FARMERS

So how did we get to the point where we are forced to be indoors at our desks on a beautiful summer day or to scramble to make it home before our kids go to sleep? Blame the farmers. Easy there, Willie Nelson—put down the hemp pitchfork. We are not talking about the family farmers of today, but rather those in the early days of agriculture.

The agricultural revolution of the eighteenth and nineteenth centuries changed two big characteristics of work. It got us out of the nomadic rat race and rooted us to a particular place, an arrangement that remains unchanged to this day with the notable exceptions of traveling sales people, carneys, and presidential candidates.

Because our farming ancestors were tied to the land, they also became tied to each other. We learned that working in groups and building long-term infrastructure for commerce has its advantages: camaraderie, mutual protection, and specialization of skills, to name a few. Figuring that little paradox out—that often the best way to serve your own selfish need for survival was to act selflessly in a group—was, in fact, a turning point for our species.

Cooperation, in fact, is the key element to our success as a species. It solved crippling problems of engineering and logistics, and the dynamic nature of mutual cooperation contributed to the growth of the human brain itself.[2] As a result mutual cooperation became encoded in all human economies in many forms. Collective farms, trade guilds, barn raisings, defense alliances, international trade, artisan colonies, sports leagues, tool co-ops, even today's open-source software are all examples of people working in groups to the ultimate benefit of the individual.

Agriculture changed everything, but the central fact of human existence remained the same. Whether hunting and gathering or growing their own food and trading the excess to neighbors in exchange for goods, our ancestors were all, in the corporate parlance of today, independent contractors. There was no such creature as the employee (although there were slaves and indentured servants). The independent yeoman farmer ideal was the basis of the romanticized Jeffersonian vision of the new American, part of the Enlightenment-inspired package of liberty on which the United States was established. This particular concept of liberty was a rebuke to the long-established feudal economies of the Old World. In 1787 Jefferson wrote to James Madison, "I think our governments will remain virtuous for many centuries as long as they are chiefly agricultural; and this will be as long as there shall be vacant lands in any part of America. When they get piled upon one another in large cities as in Europe, they will become corrupt as in Europe."[3] Whoops.

THE COMPANY

In the early nineteenth century, Jefferson's agrarian political utopia died with Jefferson himself. Agriculture became increasing mechanized, as did industry. With the rise of industrialization, the means of production became so physically enormous and so prohibitively expensive that individuals could no longer afford them. Before, a few tools, a plot of land, a bit of ingenuity, some help from your neighbor, and lots of hard work were all that you needed to make a decent living. However, as the economy became more industrialized, it demanded big machines housed in big factories, further tying people to place, because those machines needed huge amounts of resources and labor to create a finished product for the market.

Thus the company was born: a large and at times paternalistic organization that, in an echo of the feudal period, was a kind of a kingdom of its own. Instead of working for themselves, workers began to turn to the company, which gave them a highly specialized job and a salary. These companies were often brutal, and exploitative of their workers. As a result, workers rebelled, laws were enacted, and society entered the industrial era.

In hopes of pacifying their workforce out of a desire for increased profits, and a little bit of benevolence, some companies tried an approach that could easily encompass workers' lives, often providing them with housing in company-owned towns and goods in company-owned stores. Charles Eaton, an academic observer of this practice in 1894, explained that the company's responsibilities included "undertaking to house, clothe, feed, educate, and amuse the people."⁴ Following Eaton's train of thought, the company was as much a servant of the emerging social welfare state as it was a private enterprise. Today we've managed to reverse the roles, so that the state serves the interests of the enterprise. Again, don't confuse evolution with progress.

In the Gilded Age, the company took Eaton's observations and business strategy to heart. Companies were to provide good wages—because, as the industrialist Henry Ford wrote, "a low wage business is always insecure"—and improve the daily lives of their workers.[5] In a history of welfare capitalism, *Slate* magazine observed that beginning in 1914, Ford Motor Company "took steps to ensure that its employees remained healthy, loyal, and above all, efficient. It opened an infirmary and established the 'Sociological Department' to both keep tabs on and look after the welfare of its workers. In 1922, Ford cut the work week from six days to five."[6]

In the 1920s other "companies began to emulate Ford, [and] welfare capitalism began in earnest. Companies built cafeterias and health clinics, sponsored baseball and bowling leagues, and granted days off for the opening of deer season. Corning Glass Works began providing health insurance in 1923. The same year, U.S. Steel slashed its workday from 12 hours to eight. In 1927, International Harvester began offering two-week paid vacations." Other companies, like National Cash Register, went to extremes by building churches, offering dozens of classes, instituting twice-a-day calisthenics for workers and kindergarten for their children, and arranging camping and horseback trips as well as any other activity designed to increase the physical, mental, or moral strength of employees.[7]

Ironically, in the decades that followed, advances in labor rights only further tied the individual to the company with health and dental benefits, disability insurance, retirement security, paid vacations, workplace amenities, new technology, holiday parties, and, as a traditional send-off into old age, a nice engraved gold watch. Or as the sociologist C. Wright Mills explained it in his classic beach read, *The Power Elite:* "The life-fate of the modern individual depends not only upon the family into which he was born or which he enters by marriage, but increasingly upon the corporation in which he spends the most alert hours of his best years."[8]

The company became a fact of life; it changed culture in a thousand profound ways, contributing to the rise of cities, suburbs, railways, and highways, as well as to fashion, recreation, and the premise of sitcoms. A few entrepreneurial Americans challenged that system, often by going west to make their name and claim their fortune; whether during the Texas oil boom or the golden years of Hollywood, the most successful simply established themselves as the new company.

By the turn of the century, the company had achieved dominance over the nation of Jefferson. It pushed for policies that amplified its power over the economy. Compulsory public education guaranteed a steady supply of trained workers, and such laws were in force in all states by 1918. Taxes, housing, transportation, land use—all were designed to serve the rise of the company.

In return the company delivered for the United States. Powered by industrialization, fueled by abundant natural resources and a culture built around the Protestant work ethic, the United States became the wealthiest nation in the history of humankind, and today we enjoy a standard of living that is still the envy of the world. Eventually we not only exported products from cars to cola but the corporate model as well.

The price tag, however, has been considerable. The natural environment has been ravaged. Consumer culture, the rational outgrowth of industrialization, has adversely affected people's physical and spiritual well-being. Corporate influence has infiltrated our electoral processes, media, and mortgages. And you, dear reader, will work harder for less and stay at jobs you no longer enjoy because you need health insurance (if you are lucky enough to get it). At some fundamental level you have traded your Jeffersonian democratic self-determination for the (illusory) value of your 401(k) and stock options.

TRADING YOUR WATCH FOR YOUR FREEDOM

Generations of workers struck this bargain with the company, love it or hate it (or, more commonly, both), and they arrived in the twenty-first century facing an uncomfortable reality: in many important ways the company, as we have known it, is now largely becoming obsolete. We are all facing a future of no more gold watches. Right before our eyes, Jefferson's yeoman farmer is reasserting himself, except not as a farmer. The fields we will till, under new social contracts, are virtual, global, and democratic.

The funny thing is, the company never saw its demise coming. At the height of its power, American industrialism faced an existential threat in the form of Soviet-style communism, which challenged the profit-taking structure of the whole system in an argument essentially about who should own the factory. In fact, because of this very debate we designed, built, and targeted nuclear weapons that would end life-as-we-know-it.

Ironically, though, the company is being undone not by Bolsheviks in coffeehouses but by bandwidth (also largely in coffeehouses). The means of production in a knowledge-based economy are now inexpensive enough to be within the reach of the individual. All you need to work these days is a decent laptop, a fast-ish Internet connection, and some inexpensive (and increasingly free) software. No big factories, no huge capital outlays, no armies of workers.

It would be, of course, a tremendous blessing for all of us if the metamorphosis from the old economy to the new one just kind of happened overnight, like the switch to daylight saving time. But in fact this economic revolution has only just begun. If the company is disappearing, the social, political, and cultural infrastructure it leaves behind is still with us. How we work, where we live, what we eat, how we educate our children, how we spend our free time, and how we measure the health and success of our economy have all been tailored to serve the interests and metrics of the mythical company of our grandparents.

QUESTION EVERYTHING

Like government programs, cultural habits and attitudes tend to outlive their practical usefulness. Decisions made during a different period, in essentially a different world, turn into calcified traditions, and we live by them, regardless of whether there may be a better way. If there is a catchphrase for the emergence of the Naked Economy it's this: *question everything*.

The painful dislocation brought on by the collapse of the old economy is leading some workers, by choice or necessity, to examine the way they live and work. Even if not everyone recognizes the necessity, all people who work for a living need to question the structures and routines that they have, to date, taken for granted.

Somewhere along the line work and life became two different states of being, demarcated by familiar boundary lines—9 to 5, coffee breaks, quitting time, happy hour, the weekend. These rules caused many of us to live the life we wanted to live only on the margins, comfortably pursuing our true passions at night and on weekends. We became a nation of weekend warriors, cramming our hobbies, passions, and dreams into one or two days a week when those pursuits have to compete with everything from family life to romance to sleep. Even the most fundamental of human spiritual activities—thinking about God—has to conform to the structure of the work week. Increasingly, since many folks are now compelled to work at least some part of the weekend, we've given ourselves essentially one day to practice our faith, mow the lawn, get a decent bike ride in, nap, make a run to the dump, find a birthday card for our sister, take the kids to the latest Pixar masterpiece, and meditate on the secret to a happy life.

A whole lotta questioning and a little bit of technology have been liberating hundreds of millions of workers in ways that we haven't even conceived of yet. The digital revolution has turned physical stuff into data streams, yet few have really addressed the implications of that alchemy. A hundred years ago a neighborhood bank was where you stored your money and, just as important, the records of your financial activities, mostly as ink on paper in a ledger or notebook. Obviously the bank had to be located in a specific place in a specific physical building.

Today, for the great majority of us, our financial resources don't exist as tangible objects in space but as digital numbers in the cloud of cyberspace, to be accessed anywhere, given the proper level of security. We still need banks as entities for saving and investment, but as actual buildings where people work? Other than as a site for safe-deposit boxes that still hold and protect (increasingly fewer) actual things—a service that could be probably reimagined more efficiently—the answer is no, we don't need banks as places, especially when they are open only from 9 to 5 on weekdays.

And the mind-blowing thing is that this model can be applied to any number of businesses that still rent expensive office space and demand workers drive fossil fuel–spewing cars through rush-hour traffic to be physically present in that one space because that is how it has always been done.

The company is not a sentient being, some kind of mythical sea monster or vengeful demigod that demands constant placating lest it unleash pain and destruction upon the world. It's simply a mutually agreed-upon arrangement. And arrangements need periodic reassessment. The boom-and-bust madness that has characterized the US economy (and by the extension the world's) is a direct result of our workplace arrangements' being thrown out of equilibrium. A privileged minority has benefited immensely from these cycles. But most of us remain captive to an outmoded system that is keeping us on a treadmill. It has not only done violence to our 401(k)s and sense of economic justice, it continues to have an increasingly deleterious impact on our quality of life and how we spend our limited precious minutes on this earth.

History is the story of a people figuring out, when the tolerable gradually became intolerable for a critical mass of working people, how to transcend the systems that looked to be implacable and all powerful.

Have we reached another such moment in history? Isn't it about time we begin to apply the same kind of skepticism to the modern workplace? Isn't it time that, when it comes to making a living, we start to question everything?

A SHORT HISTORY OF WORK

Berries and Twigs—Free Range and Organic

Lone Mammoth Hunter—The First Entrepreneur—A Short Lived Start-up

Mammoth Hunter & Bros.—Family Business Is Born

MH Bros. Merges with Berry Farms—Mammoth Farms—Collaboration & Diversification

Royal Mammoth Farms—A Mammoth Fit for a King

Colonial Mammoth—"No Mammothization without Representation"

Mammoth Works—Industrialization of Mammoth Production

Mammoth Workers of the World Unite—Unionization

MH Inc.—Rise of the Organizational Mammoth

MH Labs—Better Mammoths through Chemistry

Mammoths 'R' Us—Mammoths—Taste Great, Less Filling . . .

MH Global—Outsourced to Cheaper Mammoth Hunters in Malaysia

MH.com—"We'll Be Bigger than Pets.com"

MH Credit Default Swaps—Backed by Collateralized Mortgages on Berries and Twigs

Stop Working for the Mammoth

CHAPTER 3

DUDE, WHERE'S MY PENSION?

Would I ever leave this company? Look, I'm all about loyalty. In fact, I feel like part of what I'm being paid for here is my loyalty. But if there were somewhere else that valued loyalty more highly, I'm going wherever they value loyalty the most.

—Dwight Schrute, *The Office*

THE PRISON BREAK

The room where Ben Gran worked had no windows. Fluorescent lights flickered overhead. His lunch breaks were short. His coworkers were angry. Rules were dictated and enforced without explanation. Gradually Ben's workplace began to remind him of other situations in which people were forced to spend their days in confined windowless spaces with their time strictly regimented by outside forces.

Ben was beginning to feel like he was doing time.

"I started having panic attacks at my desk," he said. "I kept breaking down in tears in meetings with my boss. The environment was just killing me."

To outsiders Ben had a good job as a technical writer in the regulatory compliance division of a nationally recognized bank. He had a decent salary and full health benefits. It was very much like the work environment that millions of people experience every day. But Ben felt caged.

"It was just draining me. I didn't understand why we had to be confined in this tight space when all we were doing was working on a computer. Ninety percent of what I did in my job was sending e-mails to people, most of whom were just down the hall. And that work could have all been done remotely. But the company was still stuck in this predigital mind-set of 'Well, we all have to sit here and be in one place together and have meetings about nothing of consequence.'"

That was back in 2008, when the newspapers were full of stories of a rapidly collapsing Wall Street financial industry and a newly elected president was struggling to deal with the ripple effects of what looked like a second Great Depression. Ben's wife had just had the couple's first baby. She had quit her job to stay home with the child. Ben was the sole breadwinner. "The economy was about to collapse. Everything was falling apart. And I felt existentially trapped. There just seemed to be nothing out there for me. I couldn't quit, because we needed the health insurance."[1]

Ben's experience is hardly unique, nor is it solely a product of contemporary times. But in his case, because of the rise of the Naked Economy, this story has a happy ending. It took him another year and a half of misery, but eventually he did make a transition from his soul-deadening corporate job to working as a freelance writer, making enough money to support his family. More importantly, he now enjoys a kind of freedom that, he believes, has made him a better worker and a better father and husband.

Ben Gran is now a free man.

FEAR AND LOATHING IN THE OLD SOCIAL CONTRACT

Ben's story is not just a technological one. It's tempting to say that the dazzling advances in communications technology in the last 20 years have opened up new avenues for people to work from wherever they want to work, and that's undeniably true. But Ben's experience is a good illustration of how the social contract that has bound workers and employers for generations is becoming increasingly obsolete in a world radically different from the one in which that social contract was first conceived.

In its broadest sense the "social contract" is a philosophical concept, a set of assumptions and principles recognized by both the elite and the populace at large about how civil society will work. The philosopher Thomas Hobbes believed that life is "solitary, poor, nasty, brutish, and short"; the only way to avoid anarchy was a contract in which individuals could trade some of their freedom for security.[2]

The social contract that has guided the workplace for a century, more or less, arose from the Industrial Revolution and worked for decades in an economy characterized by male-dominated, single-breadwinner households. These male breadwinners needed to gather at an appointed time and place to make the goods the world demanded. So long as labor was not too demanding, companies had a stable loyal workforce that they could manipulate for their own ends. Workers got a steady paycheck, opportunities for advancement, and benefit and retirement packages.

But the conditions, culture, and economic models that built that social contract are long gone. In the Naked Economy work is no longer a place or activity but a state of mind. Combine that reality with a brutal global economy in which corporations don't see themselves as being from a particular place or comprised of a static number of people who live in company towns, and it becomes obvious that this new economy requires completely different rules, expectations, and agreements.

A FAMILY STORY

Ben lives in Iowa, where his family has lived for generations. He was born and raised there, and after a couple of years of attending college in Texas and a year teaching English in Japan, he returned to raise a family and begin a career. In a distinctly midwestern way, Ben and his family story are also the story of the American economy and the social contract between employers and the employed as it has evolved during the last century.

His great-grandfather was a farmer in northwestern Iowa in the early part of the twentieth century, a period when farmers were nearly a third of the American labor force. The contract was simple: whatever Ben's great-grandfather produced determined his family's income and survival. There was no safety net. No Social Security. No unemployment or health insurance.

Ben's grandfather was part of the first generation of Americans to be swept up in the technological revolution of the twentieth century, becoming an industrial engineer and working for a company called Collins Radio, which began in Cedar Rapids,

Iowa, in 1933. Collins produced short-wave radio equipment and became famous the year it opened when Admiral Richard Byrd took its equipment with him to the South Pole. The company rode the postwar aerospace boom, providing voice communications equipment for the Mercury, Gemini, and Apollo space programs. It still exists today in Cedar Rapids as Rockwell Collins.

The generation of Ben's grandfather was the first to experience the 40-hour work week, and some early version of the benefits that would be become standard within a generation. Ben's father became an attorney and spent 20 years working in legal affairs for Maytag, the appliance manufacturer that was the dominant employer in Newton, Iowa, the town where Ben grew up.

The Maytag Corporation embodies the radical changes that have taken place in the American economy since the 1980s. The company, which gave the world the famous ads about the bored Maytag Repairman, had sustained a vibrant economy in Newton since the 1920s. "Maytag was, for generations, a great Iowa company," said Ben, "family-owned, paternalistic but in a good way. People called it 'Mother Maytag,' and people who worked for Maytag were very well taken care of. You just didn't have to worry. People had a nice comfortable life in a nice small town in the Midwest. You could afford a house, afford a vacation. You didn't even need a college degree. You could get a good job and support a family at Maytag." And that's what Ben's father and thousands like him did.

In 2005, however, Maytag became the subject of a corporate takeover battle, which was eventually won by Maytag's long-time rival Whirlpool. The next year—just a year shy of the hundredth anniversary of the patent for Maytag's first washing machine—the company's new owner, Whirlpool, closed the Newton headquarters. Maytag exists today only as a brand name in Whirlpool's line of appliances.

"Thousands of people in town made a living at Maytag, and now those jobs are gone," Ben said. "Newton used to be a happy place with very low unemployment, very low crime. But all that has changed. I mean, the people there are doing the best they can. But you're just not going to replace 2,000 or 3,000 good-paying blue-collar middle-class jobs like that in this economy."[3]

Maytag's retirees are still feeling the lingering aftereffects of the Maytag closure in Newton. In 2011 a federal judge ruled that Whirlpool had the right to make changes in the company's pension agreement with the union representing Maytag's retired workers.[4] The case is still under appeal, but the changes would result in retirees' having to pay more in health-care costs every year, a rewriting of the social contract that many retirees thought had been decided long ago.

This reconsideration of the social contract has played out thousands of times in communities large and small. It reflects a new corporate indifference toward workers, in combination with changing expectations of workers like Ben, who believe that they are entitled to a balanced life in which they control their time and talent. Ironically the net result is that this shift has caused Ben and his brother, who works for a nonprofit and is a farmer, to go back to their great-grandfather's social contract. They reap what they sow.

Ben's new career started under the fluorescent lights of his corporate office. Bored out of his mind, Ben picked up a stray *Newsweek* and read about freelancing as the job market of the future. He scoured the Internet for freelance writing jobs he could do in his spare time. At first he wrote at nights and on weekends, slowly building a portfolio and network. When he took family leave at the birth of his second child, he used the time to jump into freelancing full time and found that he could make more money than at his job with the bank. "The first day of full-time freelancing, I literally cried," he said. "I was overwhelmed with emotion."

Ben knows no one in Iowa who is making a living the way he is—on his own terms and under this vastly different social contract. From his home in Des Moines, Ben works with clients in Europe, Asia, Australia, and other points around the globe. For two years he has been supporting his family by working through Elance, an online employment service that links freelancers to potential clients. Ben's circle of friends and family sees his vocation as exotic.

"I've met other freelancers who work in Des Moines," Ben said, "but most of them have local clients, and some work off a few big contracts. I don't know of anyone else who just hung out a shingle on the Internet."

Ben did not end up as a freelancer for lack of other opportunities. In fact, when he walked away from that steady job at Wells Fargo, with a young child and a new baby, it was a choice based on how he wanted to live his life. He marshaled all his resources in order to take a crack at squeezing out an income on his own terms—using social networking, freelance platforms, and a small list of companies that he had worked with before. "My wife was very supportive from the beginning, and I still marvel at that," he said. "I mean, I had a solid job with benefits already. Give all that up to make money on the Internet? Who does this? My parents were kind of worried. I don't think my parents totally understood the reality of what I was able to do. It was probably strange to them."[5]

As strange as it may seem, both Ben and his brother have followed in the footsteps of their ancestors. They made choices based on the realities of the world in which they live and on the values they hold. Both have made the strategic decision to trade now-false job security from the Maytags of the world for the chance to do what they love, both for work and with their families, when they want to do it. This social contract is profoundly different from that which existed even two decades ago, but Ben and his brother are proud to be reshaping it in a way that reflects their values and aspirations.

GIRLS JUST WANNA HAVE . . . A NEW WAY TO WORK

Another major driver of this reconsideration of the old social contract is its lack of consideration for the needs of women in the workplace. And, as the nature of families has radically changed, the old social contract has shown little flexibility in adapting to new circumstances. Today women make up about 47 percent of the US workforce.[6] More than half of all women with children younger than a year old are in the workforce.[7]

What's more, women as a demographic block are not only poised to share equally in the economy but to dominate it. The news media have been awash in stories about the gender gap at colleges for more than a decade now. As the author Hanna Rosin points out in her book, *The End of Men,* it is fast becoming a woman's world.[8] Today women earn 57 percent of all undergraduate degrees and 60 percent of all master's degrees. In the 1960s women earned about 10 percent of all doctorates issued by US universities. Today that number is more than 50 percent. And though the number of women in law and medical schools still lingers at just below half of the number enrolled, the numbers are still increasing to historic levels.

Yet, despite all these advances, the wage gap between men and women, a vestige of the old social contract, persists. The Center for American Progress, a progressive think tank, reports that women still earn about 78 cents for every dollar a man earns. During a 40-year working life the average female worker stands to lose about $434,000 because of the wage gap.[9]

The social contract was forged in the days of the male breadwinner–female homemaker domestic model, which was once the most common of all domestic arrangements. Now such households make up only about 21 percent of all married households.[10] Today, although nearly three out of every four mothers of minors work outside the home, the United States is years behind Europe, Canada, and other industrialized nations in providing adequate child care, flexible work hours, and family leave.[11] Working parents in other countries still have challenges, but a fundamental policy infrastructure is in place to support families.

Child care and flexible hours were simply never factors in the old social contract, and now they are key determinants of how nearly half of all workers will decide where to deploy their talent. The White House Council of Economic Advisors considers this issue so significant to the national economy that it issued a report in 2010 entitled *Work-Life Balance and the Economics of Workplace Flexibility*. It cited a survey of 200 human resource managers who identified "family-supportive policies and flexible hours as the single most important factor"—even more than pay or benefits—in recruiting and retaining employees.[12]

THE FEE FOR BEING FEMALE

At the age of 22, in the early 1980s, Sandy Skees got her first job out of college with a small public relations firm in Cincinnati. "That was back in the day when women were wearing the menswear suits with the perky bows," she said. "So, I went out with my blue suit and my briefcase, and trying to find work was tough." At 23 she bought that same company and became an entrepreneur. It was the first of three such firms she would eventually own and manage.

A decade later, lured by the gold-rush appeal of Silicon Valley, Sandy moved to California, landing a job at a PR firm that serviced many of the high-tech businesses in the early days of the first Internet boom. At the time she was a single mom raising two daughters but soon learned that displaying pictures of your kids in your work space was frowned upon. "I had a boss who basically said, 'If I ever find out a client knows you have children, or that there's some meeting you can't make or some call you can't take, you're fired.'" That boss, by the way, was a woman.

For decades the traditional workplace maintained a kind of church-state separation between work and family. But in Sandy's case this was no old-line family business in the red-state heartland. This was Silicon Valley, in the supposedly enlightened 1990s. "People had work and play very much intermingled in Silicon Valley at the time. But they didn't have family built into it yet."[13]

The women's movement of the 1960s resulted in, among other things, a renegotiation of another social contract, this one inside the home. When middle-class wages began to flatline in the mid-1970s, the concept of women working for a salary outside the home went from an exotic lifestyle choice to an economic necessity. In the realm of family, both men and women suddenly had to reassess traditional gender roles. But even while husbands and wives were figuring out new ways to maintain a family life with both parents working, the contemporary workplace didn't seem too interested in adapting to that change.

"You couldn't leave until your boss left," said Sandy, remembering her experience of trying to be a mom to two kids while working a full-time job. "And the expectation was high that you would come in on Saturday. And it was a performance issue if you were a few minutes late and didn't stay after a particular time."

For millions of workers, raising a family necessarily had to take second place to the demands of the workplace. "It all had to be done magically behind the curtain so no one could see." Sandy gave birth twice, in 1990 and 1992. The company policy was six weeks of maternity leave—eight for women who had a caesarean section. She worked an entire year without vacation in order to add to her maternity leave. When her kid was sick, she had to take a sick day or a vacation day. "Not to mention, I'm fairly certain I was paid less than my male counterparts."

When it came to child care, she was similarly on her own. As a single mother, she had no choice but to employ a full-time day-care provider. "And essentially you're supporting two families. I had to support my own family and the nanny's family." At the same time Sandy knew plenty of other women who, in the struggle to spend more time on the family front, would talk of slowing their careers down or taking a lateral career move. These were conversations that men were not having.

Years later, Sandy found herself in a position of authority, having to address exactly these issues with a younger woman employee. "She was very ambitious and she had two little kids. And she wanted more and more work, and yet her kids were very demanding, and we had to have a hard conversation—you have to make a decision about the kind of life you want to live. For you to constantly be trying to be both an always-on mom and always-on career person, it's not working."

Sandy's advice? "My advice to men and women is that you can't have it all simultaneously. But you can have it all sequentially," and flexible work time, place, and roles are no longer to be negotiated, but are expected.[14]

RETIRING RETIREMENT?

Our culture has long sentimentalized retirement. Visions of fly-fishing in Montana, sitting on the porch with the grandkids, and strolling down the beach with your beaming gray-haired sweetheart are now solely the stuff of pharmaceutical commercials. For most of us, such visions have always seemed out of reach, but now the very notion of retirement is losing its meaning. For those who have not been able to save for it, the big question of retirement is how? But even for many who can afford it, the other big question is why?

Not only is the idea of retirement as some grand career finish line increasingly unattainable but some data suggest it is undesirable. *The Longevity Project,* a huge study of 1,500 Americans tracked from birth to death, found that one part of a long and happy life is working well past retirement age.[15] Engagement in meaningful work, even if accompanied by stress, was a strong positive indicator for longevity. "It wasn't the happiest or the most relaxed older participants who lived the longest," wrote the study's researchers, Howard Friedman and Leslie Martin. "It was those who were most engaged in pursuing their goals."[16]

The US Bureau of Labor Statistics finds that older folks are increasingly ignoring retirement. Between 1977 and 2007 the number of men 65 or older still in the workforce increased by 75 percent.[17] For women the increase was twice that. This trend is growing for economic reasons. An AARP study found that baby boomers on the edge of retirement age are quickly losing their confidence that they'll be able to retire, with more than a quarter having become more pessimistic since 2007.[18] Americans' confidence in their ability to retire comfortably is at a historic low, and a distressingly high number of people are simply not prepared for retirement, with 27 percent reporting that they have less than $1,000 in savings.[19] More than half of those surveyed don't plan to stop working.[20]

How this crisis in retirement came about is complex. But one of the dominant reasons is a fundamental change in the social contract between employers and workers. The old social contract was, in many ways, a great deal for workers. In exchange for your 35 years of toil and loyalty, you often left work with a generous pension that, coupled with equity in a house that had quadrupled in value, meant "Hello, Florida!"

But somewhere along the line those big paternalistic companies began looking for some wiggle room in their obligation to provide workers with benefit packages that promised a nice retirement. And they found it too, in the form of the "defined contribution" (DC) retirement plan, which is what economists call the 401(k)s and IRAs that most of us now depend upon for long-term savings.

The DC plan replaced the old model, the "defined benefit" (DB) pension, which was a lifetime annuity determined by a formula based on a worker's end salary and years served. It was a sweet deal for anyone healthy enough to enjoy it after four decades. But corporations determined the old DB plan, thanks to its open-ended, till-death-do-you-part nature, was a burden on their bottom line. They started looking for an out, and the DC plan was born.

In a DC plan, the employer might contribute to a retirement investment account that is largely controlled by the worker, but the growth of the plan is largely subject to the stock market. When the market is booming, everybody's happy. But in bear markets, a plan can dramatically lose value, a vagary to which the old DB model would largely have been immune. The change from DB to DC was in essence all about transferring the risk from the company to the worker.

And the tide is still going out on the worker-friendly retirement plan. From 1980 to 2008 the percentage of workers participating in DB plans fell from 38 to 20. In the same period the percentage of those in DC plans rose from 8 to 31.[21] What's more, in the wake of the 2008 Wall Street crash, many companies suspended, if not outright jettisoned, employer contributions to DC plans. In those cases the employer burden for retirement went from carrying the full weight to offering a paycheck-withholding service, a valuable courtesy but hardly a reason to stay in a job you hate or even are ambivalent about.

Philip Longman argues in the *Washington Monthly* that younger workers and women have increasingly figured this out and therefore are opting out: "Traditional benefit plans, even when well funded, were also an increasingly bad deal. Most did not offer any benefits until a worker had been with a company for at least five years, sometimes ten, and benefit formulas tended to be heavily back loaded in favor of those who spent a whole career with one company—an increasing rarity. The old pension plan system was particularly hard on women trying to combine part-time work with family responsibilities. For more and more workers, traditional pensions going forward would offer little or nothing."[22]

THE TEMP INDUSTRIAL COMPLEX

Another way of bringing down the costs of retirement benefits—and skirting the social contract for health insurance and other benefits—was to reassess the need for full-time employees altogether. Contract workers—aka "temps"—gave companies payroll flexibility as well as relief from the costs of health insurance and benefit packages. As easy as temps were to add, they were even easier to let go.

Following the recent economic downturn, the employment rate has recovered at a frustratingly slowly pace, except in one area—you guessed it—temporary workers. Between 2009 and 2012, according the Bureau of Labor Statistics, the number of temporary employees rose by 29 percent.[23] A survey of the 200 largest companies found that temporary workers represented, on average, 22 percent of their workforce . . . and that percentage is growing. Nissan, FedEx, Caterpillar, Wal-Mart, and Amazon use temps as a business strategy.[24] *Businessweek* reports that firms like Manpower, Kforce, and Kelly Staffing Services are seeing significant growth because of "robust demand" for their workers.[25] Penelope Trunk, who blogs about 20-somethings, may have said it best when she told National Public Radio that "we are increasingly becoming a nation of temps."[26]

Temporary workers are outnumbered only by part-time workers. Companies, particularly in hospitality and retail, are increasingly using part-time workers as a way to keep wages low and benefits nonexistent. The *New York Times* reported that in a 2011 survey of New York City retailers—from luxury merchants to discount stores across the city—nearly half of all retail employees were part time; only 1 in 10 had a set schedule. Carrie Gleason, executive director of the Retail Action Project, told the *Times,* "We're seeing more and more that the burden of market fluctuations is being shifted onto the workers, as opposed to the companies absorbing it themselves."[27]

THE ECONOMIC DIVIDE

Globalization has introduced American workers to intense competition and economic pressures to justify their relatively high wages. "Well, first off, as a citizen of the world, I think that everyone around the world, no matter what country they're in, should have the opportunities that we have gotten used to in the United States," Steve Miller, chair of AIG (yes, the AIG that received a multibillion-dollar bailout from US taxpayers), told Chrystia Freeland for her aptly titled book, *Plutocrats.* "Globalization is here. It's a fact of a life; it's not going away. And it does mean that for different levels of skill there's going to be a leveling out of pay scales that go with it, particularly for jobs that are mobile."[28]

This reality was captured in an eye-opening article by Charles Duhigg and Keith Bradsher of the *New York Times* about why iPhones will never be made in the United States again. In addition to describing how Chinese manufacturers can mobilize tens of thousands of workers to retool a factory overnight for a fraction of the pay that similar workers would receive in the United States, the article related that in 2011 President Obama asked Steve Jobs if Apple's products could be manufactured in the United States. Jobs's response reflected the end of the old social contract when he abruptly responded, "Those jobs aren't coming back."[29]

This has been repeated in industry after industry. Vestiges of the old social contract remain, but its core benefits were lost a long time ago. Somewhere in the mid- to late 1970s, American wages went flat. Up to that point, American workers generally enjoyed a rise in wages that exceeded the rise in the cost of living. But for 35 years now, the American worker has been largely running in place or losing ground.

Without strong government protections in place, business ran roughshod over private-sector labor unions. In 1980, about a quarter of all private-sector workers belonged to a union.[30] Today that number is 7.4 percent and continuing to head south.[31] Workers assumed that unions and government protection of middle-class incomes were part of the social contract; employers and the new conservative bloc in government were all too ready to rewrite the terms. While millions of American workers continued to work under the old arrangements, government policy was being reworked to undermine the middle class and redistribute income upward.

As a result almost all significant economic gains in growth since the early 1990s have gone to the top of the income pyramid, even as middle-class families were finding basics such as housing, health care, and education increasingly out of reach. In a shocking finding, the Nobel Prize–winning economist Joseph Stiglitz explains in his book *The Price of Inequality* that in 2010, the top one percent took 93 percent of national income and the six heirs to the Walmart fortune own as much wealth as the bottom 100 million Americans combined.[32]

Is it any wonder, then, that a recent poll by Gallup found that "53 percent of the American workforce is not engaged in their work," while a "staggering 19 percent are 'actively disengaged.'"[33] These actively disengaged workers are described by Gallup as 'CAVE Workers'—"Consistently Against Virtually Everything." We've all worked with an actively disengaged employee who is not just unhappy at work; this employee *acts out* that unhappiness. Every day actively disengaged employees tear down what their engaged coworkers are building. Sound familiar? Know that person in your business or life? Now imagine the productivity losses and general misery when that person is multiplied 20 million times—1 in every 5 American workers.

Because of the breach in the social contract, working- and middle-class people increasingly are seeing that the assumptions that they grew up with—that hard and conscientious work would inevitably lead to prosperity, that opportunity was always available to those willing to seize it, that their children would be better off than they were—are less attainable in an increasingly Darwinian economic culture. As Stiglitz notes, "There are many costs to this lack of opportunity. A large number of Americans are not living up to their potential; we're wasting our most valuable asset, our talent. As we slowly grasp what's been happening, there will be an erosion of our sense of identity, in which America is seen as a fair country. This will have direct economic effects—but also indirect ones, fraying the bonds that hold us together as a nation."[34] In other words, a contract doesn't make sense when only one side is living up to its end of the bargain.

THE NEW CONTRACT?

Seeing this inequity in wages, opportunity, and life, the political Left has offered a series of proposals. Writing for the Economic Policy Institute, Thomas Kochan and Beth Shulman captured this approach by outlining what they thought was needed to establish a new social contract between workers and employers that would reestablish a sense of opportunity and prosperity:

- Americans who work hard should have a living wage, basic health and retirement security, and the tools they need to prosper in this new economy.
- American workplaces and employment practices should support healthy and secure families rather than make workers choose between being productive workers and good family members.
- In this increasingly unstable global economy, workers must have an adequate safety net that supports workers and families as they move across jobs and/or in and out of the labor force as their life and job circumstances change over time.[35]

This sounds like a reasonable request for not only Americans, but for all workers around the globe. The problem is that these provisions are old clothes trying to find a place in a Naked Economy. Employers are unlikely, given technology, economics, and even the preferences of many of their workers, to agree. What we need is recognition of the uncomfortable truth that many aspects of the old social contract will never come back, so it's time to put a new contract in place. In *Rise of the Creative*

Class, the economist Richard Florida argues, "New ways of working have been underpinned with a new kind of employment contract. The old contract was group oriented and emphasized job security. The new one is tailored to the needs and desires of the individual."[36] This shift to an individualized social contract is essential because, he writes, "The old Organizational Age system was truly a package deal, literally a comprehensive social contract, in which people traded their working lives for money, security, and the sense of identity that came from belonging to the firm. They took their places in the hierarchy, followed bureaucratic rules, and worked their way up the ladder."[37] Instead of a broad social contract, a key feature of today's employment relationship is that employees are seeking out and getting what Carnegie Mellon professor Denise Rousseau dubbed more individualized arrangements, or "idiosyncratic deals."

Our proposed strategies and policies to rebuild the safety net and economic opportunity are coming later in Chapter 9 but first, as Florida argues, we need to recognize that a new mind-set is just beginning to be articulated in generational and gender shifts.

THE BOOMING MILLENNIAL WAY

Sandy Skees is a baby boomer. Her daughters are part of what is called the millennial generation. Boomers, she said, have played the rat-race game for years, and in midlife they've moved away from the concept of working just to acquire status or material wealth. But, she said, millennials (also called Generation Y) are arriving at the same place without that experience.

"If you think about the story that we believed, it was this series of milestones and acquisitions that defined how your life went. And I just don't see that playing out with the younger generation anymore. I don't want that in my life, and I think it's absolutely true that there are a lot of similarities between the boomers and the millennials. And I think these new attitudes are spawning an entire new way of working, a new way of living where work is not the definition of who we are anymore."[38]

At 32, Ben Gran is at the oldest edge of the millennial generation, which is increasingly shaping its experiences in the workplace to fit the new economic realities. When he remembers the time he actually made the decision to quit his full-time 9-to-5 job, he speaks not of making a transition from one mode of working to another. He talks about liberation. "I don't really want a full-time job again. I really like having my freedom, and that's worth a lot to me. The old model of a full-time job is unnecessary. If you can make this work for you, if you just keep hustling and keep the projects in your pipeline, you can make more money as a freelancer working 30 hours a week than you can working in a cubicle 40 hours a week."[39]

Get ready, employers, because you are about to have a workplace that is full of Bens—none of whom will sit at a desk just because you say so. The boomers who want or have to stay in the workplace will want only part-time work with flexible schedules to allow for travel, volunteering, and taking care of their grandkids (which will no doubt include playing Bob Dylan songs and telling bewildered five-year-olds about Woodstock). Parents will want flexible hours so that they maintain a healthy balance between work and family life. Millennials like Ben, who according to some studies will make up 75 percent of the workforce by 2025, want to work on their terms because that is the only way that makes sense to them.[40]

Ben works from home. Sometimes he goes to the public library, a coworking space, or a coffee shop in Des Moines for a change of scenery. Sometimes he blows off work altogether to take his kids to the zoo.

Sandy also works from home, in coworking spaces, and occasionally at a client's office. Her schedule reflects her focus on work but also on her family and a half-dozen charitable endeavors she is deeply committed to promoting.

In these simple life choices, Ben and Sandy reflect what the economist Sylvia Ann Hewlett and her colleagues at the Center for Work-Life Policy found in national surveys, as reported in their *Harvard Business Review* article entitled "How Gen Y and Boomers Will Reshape Your Agenda."

Their national study found that 87 percent of boomers said flexible hours at work were important to them, more important than compensation. Not a surprising demand, given the other demands on their time, including caring for their elderly parents (71 percent) and actively volunteering (55 percent).

Generation Y respondents were even more committed to the need for flexible work, with 89 percent saying it was important. And although most Gen Y-ers are mostly still in their early twenties without families, 87 percent wanted work-life balance. This led the researchers to assert:

> Stated at the highest level, our finding is that people, especially Gen Ys and Boomers, are looking for what we call a "remixed" set of rewards: Flexible work arrangements and the opportunity to give back to society trump the sheer size of the pay package. . . . This rewards remix is both challenging and liberating for talent managers. It's challenging because it means letting go of cash as the prime motivator and tangling

with the difficult task of redesigning incentives. It's liberating because if nonfinancial rewards are less expensive to fund, companies can lay out more plentiful options. Perhaps that explains why we found managers experimenting with a whole range of such rewards—figuring out how to use time, for example, as currency, or a green workplace as a retention tool.[41]

Ben Gran personifies this belief when he says: "Yeah, I don't have $10 million in the bank. But because I have this freedom, it's almost the same as being wealthy. If you have the freedom and you can do what you want with your day, then that's worth a lot. I still sometimes feel that I can't believe I'm getting away with this."[42]

PART II

A SPECIALIST AND GENERALIST WALK INTO A BAR . . . GET DRUNK, AND START A COMPANY

Prospering in the New Economy

CHAPTER 4

IF YOU ARE SPECIAL AND YOU KNOW IT . . . GET NAKED

If a man can write a better book, preach a better sermon, or make a better mousetrap than his neighbor, though he build his house in the woods, the world will make a beaten path to his door.

—Henry David Thoreau

SUPER SPECIAL SPECIALISTS SPECIALIZE

As a kid during frequent visits to the Chesapeake Bay, Wallace J. Nichols dreamed of turtles. Or at least he stayed up nights thinking about them. "There was something about their shape that really got under my skin and invaded my mind. Call it spiritual, call it something else, but to this day, I see turtles where there aren't turtles. I see turtle-shaped things. It's sort of an obsession but definitely not the worst kind."[1]

Today he is Dr. Wallace J. Nichols—to his friends, he's just "J."—a research associate at the California Academy of Sciences, founder and director of several ocean advocacy programs, one of the leading voices of ocean conservation on the West Coast, and a go-to source for the national media on issues of marine wildlife. But if you ask him what he does, J. will often just say, "I save turtles." That's a simple declarative sentence— a long-standing passion combined with a highly specialized niche that he has translated into a life and a living.

Welcome to the Age of the Super Specialist, a key player in the Naked Economy. Specialists of all kinds have existed for millennia, from the guy who could make the best spear points to the woman who can write the most complicated software. In fact our ability to specialize and trade that expertise with other specialists is the very foundation of our society, economy, and culture. Way back in 1952, the German philosopher Josef Pieper laid out this idea in his book *Leisure, the Basis of Culture.* In case you chose to read the Harry Potter books instead, Pieper's insight was that with increased specialization, individuals no longer needed to do everything themselves in order to survive. Banding together with other specialists meant pooling talent to tackle increasingly complex problems. It also meant that many of us now had one of the most precious commodities ever discovered: free time. And with that free time we got into all sorts of mischief, from pondering the vagaries of life through art, poetry, and song to engaging in a wide array of political punditry or overeating, oversleeping, and overromancing. Our ability to specialize is also what gives rise to modern diversified economies. I can get really good at creating iPhone apps and let someone else worry about growing my food, building my house, and keeping me entertained playing Angry Birds.

But here's the thing: in a globalized, connected economy, specialists are no longer very special. Can you write computer programs? Great, so can several million other people around the world. Is creating legal documents your thing? That's a bummer because a dozen different software programs can do the same job you can, not to mention the throngs of highly skilled, low-paid workers in developing countries who are eager to steal all your business away from you. What's more, the prevalence of search engines, social media, and inexpensive communications technology has made the task of engaging with these specialists an increasingly frictionless process. With a few clicks of a mouse, companies can find exactly the person with precisely the skills they need, whether that person is in Brooklyn, Bangladesh, or Berlin. A few e-mails and maybe a couple of Skype conversations are all it takes to connect with and contract for the specialized talent that they're looking for. And new companies are being formed to provide online platforms that allow for easy management, billing, and payment for such transactions. Specialists and tools to find them are now a dime a dozen.

The answer to this new set of circumstances is actually quite simple: Specialists need to become more specialized around defined specialized tasks. Indeed, the specialist needs to become a Super Specialist, a person who possesses skills and talents so unique that he, quite literally, is the only person on the entire planet who can do what he does. Then, using the global marketing reach and personal brand-building tools that are now available to individuals—things like blogs, Twitter, and Facebook—these Super Specialists must communicate their skills and talents to a global audience. The idea is not to be just a software programmer but to be one of only a few people who can apply a specific software program to a highly specific problem. Or a lawyer who can create legal documents around a specific set of circumstances. If these Super Specialists are marketing to seven billion potential customers, odds are they'll be able to find more than enough customers without having to worry much about the competition. If they can do these two things—find a niche and then tell the world about it—the Super Specialists will be able to name their price as key players in the Naked Economy.

THE SUPERSPECIALIZED TURTLE CHASER

So let's return to the story of J. and the turtles. When J. was about ten, he began catching snapping turtles with his friends near his home, marking the turtles' shells with a number, and releasing them again. What started as a lark turned into an obsession. "We'd catch them again and be really amazed and excited when one showed up with one of our numbers on it," he said. "We'd pretend we were scientists and do some simple algebra and calculate their population size. Of course we were just kids and had no idea what we were doing. But we felt like there was a bigger mystery that we were trying to unravel, something really exotic and secret. Where's that turtle been? Is it still alive? Did it move from where it had originally come from? And where is it going?" Just as other kids had baseball cards or skateboards, J. had turtles.

His interest in turtles led him eventually to Duke University, where he got a master's degree in economics and environmental policy and later to the University of Arizona, where he earned his PhD in wildlife ecology and evolutionary biology. However, J. said that he went through much of his academic career feeling disconnected from his tenure-minded peers. To escape books and labs he supplemented his academic work by spending months working with impoverished turtle catchers in Mexico and living out of the back of his truck. He figured understanding the biology of turtles wouldn't help save them if he didn't also understand the economic and cultural pressures on humans, the turtles' biggest predators. This passionately interdisciplinary approach and a deep understanding of all aspects of his field are what kept J. on the path toward superspecialization.

Moreover, J. wanted to play on a bigger stage than what academia offers. He questioned everything about the approach that seemed to value research over results. He knew that he and his turtles had a special story to tell and that the world needed to hear it. "People in a position to help me and mentor me in academia were openly confused by what I was trying to accomplish. They'd tell me just to do my research, write my academic articles, get a pat on the back at the next conference, and everything would be fine," he said. "But I saw myself as someone who could solve problems, maybe even big problems. I liked the idea of doing whatever it took to solve those problems. And I wanted to communicate to a much bigger audience."

So J. broke all the rules of academia, where jealously guarding your data and staying cloistered within the ivory tower were the cardinal rules. Instead he began using new communications technology to start telling the world about turtles. He first made his name as a scientist in the mid-1990s when he put a transmitter on a female turtle he named Adelita. Far from keeping his work secret, he recruited the commercial fishermen he got to know in the Gulf of California—considered the enemy by many wildlife biologists—to help him track turtles. In the early days he used fax machines—high-tech gear at the time—to share his data among his many contacts.

In 1996, during the early years of the Internet, J. began putting his data online. "All my colleagues were shocked that I would share my data in real time. Academics never do that, for fear of being scooped. Well, if my goal is to save turtles and someone steals my data in order to . . . save turtles, why wouldn't I do that?" J. said with a smile. "That's why I shared the data as widely as possible, and soon I was getting coverage on CNN and National Geographic. And before long, millions of people found this turtle and they could track it. Adelita ended up traveling from Baja California all the way across the Pacific Ocean to Japan. People—regular, nonacademic people—were fascinated. And suddenly millions more people cared about turtles." Using these new communications tools to tell a global audience about his passion for saving turtles, J. stood as an early example of how a Super Specialist can use a globalized, connected economy to his and his cause's advantage.

Nearly twenty years later, J. continues his work as a turtle Super Specialist. No one else on the planet possesses the depth and breadth of knowledge that J. does about turtles and is able to communicate with a global audience about how regular people fit into the larger science of marine conservation. His work lands him on television, gets him cited in the popular and academic press, gets him invited to the best universities in the world to lecture. If you want to know about turtles, there's literally no one better in the world than J., our superspecialized turtle guy.

THE AGE OF SUPERSPECIALIZATION

If the new globally connected world has utterly transformed academic and specialty interests, imagine what it's done to the workplace and the talent market. In the nineteenth century, before the invention of the locomotive and the telegraph, information could travel only as fast as any human or animal could carry it. Similarly, in the pre-Internet age specialized talent could find work only within a radius of a reasonable daily commute. As the Internet has made the exchange of work and compensation in many arenas a global phenomenon, specialization in the workplace is quickly evolving into even more narrow categories.

The new world of superspecialization is not only a boon for workers with specialized skills that they can now market globally but also a potential benefit for companies looking to be more efficient in performing specific tasks. Companies now have more freedom than ever to tap into talent markets for "supertemps," specialized workers who can perform one narrow job without a long-term commitment from either side.[2] And the economics of such a situation drives both companies and specialists to find each other. A specialist can be paid a handsome fee and, compared with the costs of training full-time employees or the costs of bringing in a big consulting firm, the company can still come out ahead.

The MIT management professors Thomas W. Malone and Robert J. Laubacher, and Tammy Johns, an executive with a staffing firm, report their extensive study of this phenomenon in "The Age of Hyperspecialization."[3] They cite as an example a law firm that is sending junior associates to research some tiny slice of arcane law, when the same firm could turn around and bring in a for-hire specialist in that specific area of law: "It could pay a hyperspecialist five times the hourly rate of a junior associate and still come out well ahead on costs." Take this small example and replicate it millions of times in industries as varied as medicine, programming, manufacturing, design, and marketing, and we are talking about a big change. "Today, thanks to the rise of knowledge work and communications technology, this subdivision of labor has advanced to a point where the next difference in degree will constitute a difference in kind. We are entering an era of hyperspecialization—a very different, and not yet widely understood, world of work," Malone and his colleagues wrote. "We envision the emergence of a rich ecosystem—for-profit firms, government agencies from many nations, and nonprofits, all governed by global rules and standards—to support hyperspecialization. It would be much like today's web, except that instead of enabling the exchange of information and goods, it would convey a pulsating, world-spanning flow of knowledge work."[4]

The pharmaceutical company Pfizer took on the task of figuring out what small tasks it was paying too much for with an initiative called PfizerWorks. After surveying its staff, Pfizer figured out that its most highly skilled technological workers were spending 20 to 40 percent of their time on such tasks as data entry, web research, and PowerPoint slides—all tasks that they could easily farm out to less expensive freelancers who specialized in this sort of work. Moreover, by freeing their employees from these more mundane tasks, Pfizer created an opportunity for its highly skilled workers to become even more specialized and even better at the job they were being paid to do.[5]

Into this new dynamic comes talent brokers like Jody Greenstone Miller, the cofounder and CEO of the Business Talent Group (BTG), a firm that places specialized talent with companies and organizations to work on specific projects. Jody and her cofounding business partner, Amelia Warren Tyagi, established BTG with venture capital financing and advice from some of the biggest names in business and government. BTG helps businesses with the tasks for which the big consulting firms were unsuitable—too unwieldy or expensive—and plays matchmaker for highly skilled professionals looking for a bit of flexibility in their work lives.

"If you think about the life of a consultant in particular," Jody said, "they walk in Monday morning, and they're told to go to Timbuktu for six months, and they don't have a lot of choice about it. I think the firms are trying to be a bit more responsive to that, but it's hard because the basic business model of the top consulting firms is the premium pricing to do exactly that, to field high-class teams, immediately, globally." Instead, BTG matches clients and talent on a smaller scale, with more value for the clients and more control for the talent.

Jody has led a wildly varied career, from public policy to commercial media. On the political side, she worked in the Department of the Treasury under President George H. W. Bush and was a White House special assistant to aide David Gergen during the Clinton administration. She also worked as legal counsel to South Carolina governor Richard Riley. In the private sector she served as vice president, and later as acting president of Americast, the Walt Disney Company's digital television initiative; her job was building partnerships with various telecommunications companies. She had also done several stints as a project-based consultant and was working for the venture capital firm Maveron when the idea of BTG first came to her. She found that she could assemble small teams of highly skilled people to take on projects for which the bigger firms weren't necessarily suitable.

"The clients were telling me, 'This is amazing. This doesn't exist anywhere else. And it's a third of the price.' And the talent was very happy, too. They were thrilled to be paid a decent amount of money to work on projects that they found interesting." Only then did Jody start to see the emergence of an enormous, largely untapped, workforce of highly skilled professionals who were looking for quick but challenging specialized projects in a specific time frame.

"What I was essentially doing was finding amazing people with highly specialized skills who were interested and available for project-based work and bringing them fabulous opportunities. What I learned is that I could pay them the same amount, and often a higher amount, than they were making when they were at these firms, take something for my efforts, and still be a third of the price and [provide] a better product."[6]

Such talented consultants, she said, were happy to do certain kinds of highly specialized projects, but they rarely had the means or the interest to seek them out. On other side of the transaction, she thought of the many times she needed a particular job done but felt trapped by the options of bringing in a permanent employee or hiring a multimillion-dollar consulting firm.

But Jody had a good gig at Maveron and wasn't particularly excited about taking on the demands of a start-up in an unproved market. She looked to the British firm of Eden Mc-Callum, which was doing something similar in Europe, where antiquated labor laws had inadvertently created a huge market for temporary skilled workers. Her idea was to collect a stable of top business talent, including a core group of experienced consultants, as well as some unattached executives, to create a "new kind of product in the market." In other words, she wanted to create a superspecialized temp agency.

It turned out to be a good call. Since Business Talent Group opened for business in 2007, the company has achieved consistent growth, Jody said. Today BTG has offices in New York, Los Angeles, the San Francisco Bay Area, and Austin, with Chicago opening soon. The recession of 2008 ultimately helped the company because potential clients, faced with reduced resources and an uncertain future, became more open to experimenting with different ways of using labor and work arrangements.

"Companies are more and more breaking down the work that needs to be done, and this is the key thing that has to happen for the Super Specialists to really take charge," Jody said. "They have to [learn to] say, not 'I need a head of marketing'—they need to say, 'I need someone to come in and undertake the highly specialized task of, say, redoing a loyalty program.' They need to break down the work into doable, measurable work products, and as they do that, project-based work will explode."[7]

Julie Gupta is one of the specialist talents Jody recruited for BTG early on. Julie works as an independent consultant, taking occasional projects from BTG when she isn't working on her own projects. She is representative of the kind of people who don't fit the stereotype of a temp. Educated at MIT and Harvard Business School, she has worked for IBM, Bain, AOL, and Sun Microsystems.

If Julie had stayed in the corporate world, she figured, she would likely be a partner in a firm today. Though she said she makes a good living, many in her peer group, she believes, make significantly more money. But she has reasons for remaining a free agent. She knows that the life of a well-paid consultant at McKinsey or Bain can be a brutal one. Her life, in contrast, is on her terms.

"When you're at a Bain or a McKinsey, you take what comes your way. You generally don't get to choose your clients," she noted. Running her own shop, she gets to travel and follow her off-the-clock interests, from piano to yoga to diving. "I have time for social activities. I have time for the gym. I'm able to take off large chunks of time if I want to."[8]

Life as a supertemp has given Julie the freedom to pursue other avenues in her life. And being associated with BTG allows her to focus on the job at hand and not be constantly on the prowl for new business before the job in front of her is finished. She is, she said, a passionate traveler, and she has been known to take jobs for the experience of living in a different culture. "I had a chance to work for a year in Malaysia and thought, well, why not?" She is now trying out New York. Her freelancing has also enhanced her interpersonal and family relationships. "It's been useful. At my parents' age, it's nice for me to have that flexibility to be able to check out for a couple of months if I need to be with them, even if they don't quite get what I do for a living," she said.[9]

Jody Miller said that her consultants appreciate the lifestyle, but mostly they are "people who like the adrenaline of going into something new, solving a highly specialized problem, then coming out. That's just what they like to do."[10] In the Naked Economy, the firms that succeed will be those that are able to attract the Super Specialist with that value proposition: solve an interesting problem on terms that work for your life.

THE MICROWORKERS

Not everyone, however, comes into the market for superspecialized freelance talent carrying a Harvard Business School degree. The BTG model is just one model emerging as companies explore new ways to engage workers. One alternative model comes from a company called TopCoder, a Connecticut-based software firm that takes its clients' IT jobs and carves them up into small pieces, creating tiny discrete jobs for the software coders in its talent base. The coders then compete for the right to attack each piece, and their reputations grow with each challenge that they successfully complete. Such a model rewards those who can burrow deep into a project and become especially good at one specific service or task. The economies of scale that TopCoder has set up, serving clients from a pool of potential customers that is global in size, means that TopCoder can pay its coders well and still make money for the company overall.

CastingWords, an audio transcription service, is another example of a company built on using flexible, highly specialized microworkers. Dissatisfied with the quality of transcriptions created by software, which often missed colloquialisms and arcane words, Nathan McFarland, a cofounder of CastingWords, knew he needed an army of highly skilled transcribers who could work on specific tasks. He found them through Amazon's Mechanical Turk, a service that matches freelance workers with discrete "human intelligence tasks," or HITs. As the name suggests, these tasks require real, live, thinking humans to complete. And these humans succeed when they become good at one specific thing, like audio transcription, and sell that talent to the highest bidder. McFarland says that workers on Mechanical Turk "like specialization. They like to do one task they do very well and just keep doing it. If they find a HIT they like, they will come back day after day."[11] CastingWords and Mechanical Turk show that you don't need a PhD to succeed in the Age of the Super Specialist. You just need to find something you're really good at and sell that talent in the global marketplace.

PROJECTS ARE REAL JOBS

However, old habits die hard, and many companies are reluctant to abandon the idea that the only way to get top talent into a company is through an employee-based model. "The world is really bifurcated on this issue right now," said BTG's Jody Miller about the struggle to convince companies to outsource some of their work to the growing army of Super Specialists. "A few companies truly understand that there are great people in this sector of the workforce, and by aggressively utilizing this workforce, they can get great results cost-effectively. Yet for most companies, this new reality feels foreign and unfamiliar and they're skeptical about the talent pool."[12]

This suspicion about using specialized consultants and freelancers—whether they're low skilled or high skilled—stands as an enormous barrier to the widespread adoption of super-specialized talent. Too often, said Jody, the rest of the business world sees consultants as high-priced hired guns who don't deliver much value. She's often faced with the challenge of convincing companies that BTG is not a traditional consulting firm. The average costs for one of BTG's projects is in the neighborhood of six figures, while the typical cost of an engagement with Bain or McKinsey can run well into seven or even eight figures. Where a big firm might bring in a five-person team, BTG will insert one or two people in the mix, causing much less wear and tear on the client company. Paradoxically, companies often feel like they're not getting their money's worth unless they're spending a lot of money.

This paradox illuminates a troubling bias that Super Specialists, consultants, and freelancers must overcome if they want to be successful in the Naked Economy: the notion that truly talented people have "real jobs" while those who can't hack it in a real job have no recourse except to become consultants. "Potential client companies often have a knee-jerk reaction that our talent can't be that good if they're not in high-paying permanent jobs," Jody noted. Thankfully her firm is on the vanguard of erasing that bias. "I really think those old notions are slowly giving way. Once companies have some exposure to our firm, and to firms like ours, they quickly realize that we deliver extremely high quality at very reasonable prices."[13] So the shift toward favoring Super Specialists on a project-by-project basis has begun.

Sustaining that shift is a tougher sell. But companies are beginning to understand the value of this shift as it begins to impact their bottom lines. When companies identify a specific need in their organization and choose to fill it with an employee, that's an expensive proposition, particularly if the need is a specialized one. Employees need to be recruited, brought on board, and trained before they can begin to be effective in an organization. That process takes time and costs money. And as the war for talent heats up, not much stops those employees from walking out the door to seek a new opportunity, taking all that time, money, and training with them. From this perspective it's easy to see why companies find Super Specialists appealing. Super Specialists deliver precisely the talent needed. And because they're often willing to work flexibly as freelancers or consultants, they can deliver the exact dose of talent needed. As companies get better at using this kind of talent, and as Super Specialists get better at delivering it, they combine to create a real win-win, keeping the companies' costs low and the specialists' fees high. These win-wins will sustain this new Age of the Super Specialist.

FINDING ANGELS

For all the promise that being a Super Specialist offers, one drawback is significant: the lack of stability that a "real job" with a regular paycheck offers. While the demand for superspecialized talent is real, it's not always constant. And finding creative ways to bring in money during lean times is still an important ancillary skill that Super Specialists need to have. Which brings us back to J. Nichols, our celebrity turtle specialist.

Much like Julie Gupta and other professionals who could follow a more lucrative traditional career path but choose to remain independent, J. has found that his independence comes with a price. For a while, he was indeed drawing a salary at the nonprofit Ocean Conservancy in Washington, DC, trading a little bit of his intellectual freedom for the security of a regular paycheck. But then he began talking about the plastics that form enormous garbage patches in the oceans and threaten the health and lives of all sorts of marine animals, including his beloved turtles. Some funders of that organization had created those plastics and weren't too keen about J. dissing their companies. He began to feel a subtle but real pressure to keep quiet. Rather than muzzle himself, he decided to quit. "I came home, after walking away from that salary and that stability, and told my wife, Dana, about my reasons for leaving. And she asked a great question: 'Good move . . . now what?'"

To continue to do his work on behalf of sea turtles and the oceans, J. came up with an innovative idea he calls "100 Blue Angels." It is similar to the increasingly popular online crowdfunding site Kickstarter. But where Kickstarter funds individual discrete projects, 100 Blue Angels is designed to be an ongoing source of funding for J. and his work. "The idea is to find

100 people who are willing to donate monthly to a fund," J. explained. "My pitch to them is simple. I tell them what I've done in the past and the impacts I've made around this idea of marine conservation. And here's what I want to do in the future. Becoming one of my Blue Angels gives them an opportunity to participate, often in small ways, to sustain this work."[14]

The Blue Angels project is still a work in progress. "It hasn't totally come together yet, but it's getting close to allowing me to focus on my specialty and my passion," he said. "But I'm still running around doing side things that I would rather not be doing in order to bring in extra income." Of course those side things don't sound so bad. J. gets paid to speak at conferences, assist with grants, and write for a few online outlets. And he's even modeled for The Gap. But the early success of the Blue Angels is a huge step toward allowing him to focus 100 percent of his time on his specialty and his passion.

Buoyed by his progress, J. has begun teaching this crowd-funding model to colleagues as a way to augment the foundation- and government-sponsored grants that typically fund academic research projects. He feels that direct connections with the public through these crowd-funding efforts give people an everyday stake in field research in a way that they don't when big funders provide the money. "People need to feel that when I'm getting on a plane to Honduras to participate in a field research project, they're getting on a plane to Honduras, too."

Efforts such as J.'s Blue Angels would have been unlikely, if not impossible, in a pre-Internet age, but he has worked hard to maximize the modern tools of connectivity—social media, blogs, YouTube, and Skype—to fashion a highly specialized spot for himself in the global economy. This approach allows him to do serious research, maintain his independence to advocate on various issues, and keep body and soul together. In fact J. is a self-described introvert. He is happy to undertake the high-energy publicity efforts that are required to keep his work in the forefront of public consciousness. But the flexibility and independence that are part and parcel of his superspecialization also allow him time to retreat to his home, surf, and spend time with his family. "I just get wiped out, so eventually I'm able to come up the coast and down the road and just hibernate for a bit to get recharged and get back out there again to do what I love to do. It's the career everybody would have, or would want to have."

Though J. acknowledged he's hardly living in the lap of luxury—he and Dana and their two daughters live in a rural area along California's wide-open "Slow Coast" south of San Francisco—he said he has become an unlikely role model for younger would-be researchers. "There are people getting their PhDs in my field [who are] now coming to me and saying, 'I don't know how you created your career, but I want to do something like it, because this gig I'm being offered at Stanford, which used to be the dream job in the dream lab at the dream university, well, it's just not very exciting.'"

So he's become what he himself could not find years ago, an informal mentor. "When people say to me, 'What is it you do and how do I get that?' my first question to them is, 'How do you feel about living in a yurt, eating almonds and avocados for a little bit, or a long time?' It's really the start-up mentality. If you're willing to work out of a garage and sleep on someone's couch, you can start things up. That applies to environmental science just as it applies to everything else."[15]

Like much in the new Naked Economy, the path to being a successful Super Specialist—or, for companies, to effectively use Super Specialists—is still being blazed by brave souls like J. Nichols, Jody Miller, and Julie Gupta. As we've shown, they've got their work cut out for them as they attempt to convince the world that their model holds enormous promise, both for companies that use Super Specialists and for the Super Specialists themselves. Ultimately, we think, these benefits will be the driving force behind the widespread adoption of this model. Companies will gain access to exactly the talent they need in exactly the dose that they need it. And Super Specialists will get to ply their skills in a manner that allows them to make a living without sacrificing their ability to lead a life. A rare win-win in a cutthroat economy. In the next several chapters, we'll show that quest for balance in all sorts of weird and wonderful ways.

CHAPTER 5

THE GENERALLY BRIGHT FUTURE FOR SMART GENERALISTS

An idea is always a generalization, and generalization is a property of thinking. To generalize means to think.
—Georg Wilhelm Friedrich Hegel

THE GENERALISTS' GENERAL

Everyone who has ever faced a problem that calls for an immediate solution—be it a refrigerator on the fritz, an impacted wisdom tooth, or a nuclear power plant on the verge of melting down—understands the appeal of the expert. If you're building your dream home, facing heart surgery, or dreaming up an idea for a killer smart phone app, you want as much expertise on your side as you can afford.

The appeal of the generalist—that is, the big-picture thinker who can synthesize multiple perspectives and who is the complement to the Super Specialists we met in Chapter 4— is a harder sell. In a way this is understandable. In the industrial economy and in the information-technology economy, we've needed and valued deep, specialized knowledge. The guy fixing the brakes on your car, the woman operating on your heart, or the team writing the software that makes the electrical grid function had better know what they're doing. The last thing we need these people to be doing is talking philosophy and worrying about "the big picture." It's also easier to get our heads around the appeal of specialists because we can usually measure the results of their work, often with great precision: the brakes make your car stop, your heart is still ticking, and electricity is available to power your new 90-inch flat screen TV. The talents and the results produced by generalists are difficult, if not impossible, to measure with any kind of precision. Which, if you think about it, is kind of the point.

Still, in a world still dominated by the Super Specialists, the appeal of generalists is gaining some traction. Dr. Liz Coleman, for one, is a champion of the generalist. To Coleman, we have wandered too far down the path to narrower and narrower specialization. Sure, we may know more and more about the trees than we ever have. But we've utterly forgotten to look at the forest.

Coleman is president of Bennington College, a small liberal arts school in Bennington, Vermont. In that position she has taken it upon herself to become one of the most passionate voices in defense of both the utility and the grandeur of the generalist mind-set. To Coleman the difference between the expert and the generalist is largely the difference between training and education. Ironically, in her expert super specialist opinion, we have too much of the former and simply not enough of the latter.

For years, Coleman has been a controversial figure in higher education. In 1993, she eliminated tenure at Bennington and fired a third of its professors. She has long lamented the balkanization of academic disciplines: "Subject matters are broken up into smaller and smaller pieces, with increasing emphasis on the technical and obscure," she said to the TED Conference in a 2009 talk. Nor has she been averse to the sweeping pronouncement: "In truth, liberal arts education no longer exists—at least genuine liberal arts education—in this country."[1]

And that's too bad. For centuries the classic liberal arts education—a balance of literature, philosophy, hard science, and social science—was one of the key underpinnings of our society. A liberal arts education didn't provide many answers. Instead the point of a liberal arts education was to provide a common framework and a common lexicon within which we create answers and solutions to the ever-shifting challenges and opportunities we face as a society. E. D. Hirsch, in his groundbreaking 1987 book *Cultural Literacy,* wrote about this idea with a great deal of eloquence and urgency, presaging some of the economic challenges we face in the early twenty-first century. Hirsch described cultural literacy as the "network of information" that all competent people in a society possess. For Hirsch, this cultural literacy is absolutely essential for our society to survive and thrive. He notes, "The complex undertakings of modern life depend on the cooperation of many people with different specialties in different places. Where communications fail, so do the undertakings."[2] In essence, Hirsch is arguing for exactly what the Smart Generalist offers: the broad knowledge—knowing a little bit about a lot of things—that is the glue that holds the work of the Super Specialists together so that we can indeed succeed in the complex undertaking to which Hirsch alludes. So we need the Smart Generalists now, perhaps more than ever. Our friend Liz Coleman of Bennington College thinks she knows how to make them.

THE MAKING OF A GENERALIST

The question of generalists in the new economy is much more than just pondering whether English and philosophy majors have a place in a high-tech globalized world. It's really about whether the specialist and the generalist can understand and respect the unique perspective each brings to the world. Expertise will always be needed. But in the new economy experts must exist in harmony with those with a gift for strategic thinking, critical reasoning, and connecting the dots.

In addressing the question of generalists, it is important to return to the ideas of Coleman and soar in the rarefied air of educational theory for a bit. Coleman would be the first to remind you that education has, for most of human history, been prized exactly because of its broadness and applicability to a wide number of human questions. It wasn't until the industrial age that specialization in technical skills became a kind of parallel mode of education. In fact a watershed moment may have occurred sometime in the twentieth century when a philosophy major approached her father with her new degree, and her father skeptically asked that now-familiar question: "So what kind of job is reading Plato going to get you?"

Today, of course, with tuition soaring, philosophy majors are often viewed as unemployable eccentrics, and that's putting it generously. The justification of a broad general liberal arts education has begun to fade behind the demand for ever-increasing levels of specialization. In a world that makes widgets doesn't it make sense to learn everything you can about widget making and save the Jane Austen novels for the weekend?

This idea is so pervasive that it is no wonder Coleman's views have taken a while to gain traction. "Our public education, once a model for the world, has become most noteworthy for its failures," she said at the 2009 TED conference. "Mastery of basic skills and a bare minimum of cultural literacy eludes vast numbers of our students. Despite having a research establishment that is the envy of the world, more than half of the American public doesn't believe in evolution. And don't press your luck about how much those who do believe in it actually understand it."[3]

It's hard to argue with Coleman's grim assessment, but she is not engaging in empty criticism of academic bureaucracy. She is issuing a call to arms that says the issues that have plagued American democracy in recent decades—apathy and indifference to social action, as well as divisiveness and demagoguery, and the assault on constitutional values, among others—are rooted in the failures of the educational system. "No one is drawing any connections between what is happening to the body politic, and what is happening in our leading educational institutions. We may be at the top of the list when it comes to influencing access to personal wealth. We are not even on the list when it comes to our responsibility for the health of this democracy," Coleman said. "We are playing with fire. You can be sure Jefferson knew what he was talking about when he said, 'If a nation expects to be ignorant and free in a state of civilization, it expects what never was, and never will be.'"[4]

Coleman's response to the sad state of affairs she outlines could have profound effects not only on the future of civic life but on the future of the workplace. She spearheaded efforts to build the Center for the Advancement of Public Action (CAPA) at Bennington, a kind of generalist seed bed whose curriculum is steadfastly built around the problems the world faces, including poverty, war, environment degradation, public health crises, the struggle for democracy, and the state of education itself.

This problem-based approach is beginning to take hold at educational institutions around the world. For example, the core graduate courses at Yale's School of Management don't cover accounting, finance, marketing, and the like—the core topics taught at business schools of yesteryear. Certainly, these specialized courses are part of the curriculum. But the core is built around a series of interdisciplinary courses called "Organizational Perspectives" that "teach students to draw on a broad range of information, tools, and skills to develop creative solutions and make strategic decisions," according to the business school's website. The goal is for Yale's graduate students in business to understand how the internal aspects of a business—such as operations, human resources, and finance—affect a broad range of external stakeholders, including customers, the environment, the macro economy, and society as a whole. Knowing a little about all these things is the key to being successful a leader and the hallmark of the Smart Generalist.

Coleman does not denigrate the need for specialization. But, she said, "this single-mindedness will not yield the flexibilities of mind, the multiplicity of perspectives, the capacities for collaboration and innovation this country needs." At another conference in 2010 she spoke of the "fundamentalism about expertise" that has dominated educational thought for 150 years.[5] She said that expertise is essential in making sure "the building doesn't fall down, but that is very different from thinking that the only model of serious accomplishment, the only model of a serious education, is one in which you become progressively more sophisticated about something narrower and narrower."

The course catalogue for CAPA at Bennington reflects Coleman's generalist worldview. It includes courses on interpreting data; the social action aspects of media; rhetoric; "How to Read a Poem," the art of critiquing; and even something called "Aphorism: From Ideas to Action," a forum for exploring those bite-sized pieces of wisdom we usually see on bumper stickers. None of these courses leads to any kind of expertise, as we understand that term. Instead they underline CAPA's primary mission, which is to address three fundamental questions: What kind of world are we making? What kind of world should we be making? What kind of world can we be making? The Smart Generalist, often analyzing and synthesizing the work of the Super Specialist, is best equipped to answer these questions.

THE PAYING OF A GENERALIST

But what does a generalist education get you in the commercial world? Potentially quite a lot. Or so says research by Rice University's D. Michael Lindsay, who studied the financial elite in the United States.[6] Lindsay interviewed 500 of America's elite in a variety of fields and found that privileged upbringings and elite schools were quite common among the wealthy and certainly contributed to their success. But the key to their success, Lindsay found, was that most of these successful people had a generalist mind-set. Lindsay's interview subjects said being able to resist the call to dive into a specialty and instead adopt a generalist's approach brought them into leadership roles early in their careers. "These people had a chance to be a generalist early on, as opposed to being a specialist their whole careers," Lindsay told the *New York Times*.[7] At a gathering on the future of work at the Aspen Institute in 2011, Maryam Alavi, vice dean of the Goizueta Business School at Emory University and holder of the John and Lucy Cook Chair of Information Strategy, explained why these skills are increasingly relevant: "Beyond cognitive competencies, there is a whole arena of emotional intelligence. This involves knowing one's self, being able to self-manage, being able to connect to others and being able to show empathy toward others. There are also competencies around social relations that relate to teamwork, negotiation and conflict management. And then there are behavioral competencies that involve our actions." In short, the work of the future will require much more holistic thinking.

"The most effective individuals," Alavi continued, "are those who have a well-rounded development of these sets of skills, and they know which ones to apply. In fact, there are some newer studies of brain imaging that show that very effective strategic thinkers fire on various parts of the brain related to these different sets of competencies."[8]

In his book *Elsewhere U.S.A.* Dalton Conley of New York University makes the case for generalists: "Jobs created over the last 40 years have not gotten more specific; they have actually gotten broader. . . . Computers have taken over many rote tasks, and instead, we need to be able to synthesize, process, and draw abstractions from the increasing amounts of data that are presented to us."[9]

And, as far as that much-maligned liberal arts education goes, an educational policy study issued by the Social Science

Research Council and the Collegiate Learning Association put some oomph into Liz Coleman's faith in the liberal arts. "Improving Undergraduate Learning," by Richard Arum, Josipa Roksa, and Esther Cho, found that students majoring in traditional liberal arts subjects demonstrated significantly higher gains in critical thinking, complex reasoning, and writing skills over time than students in other fields of study. Of course, in this respect liberal arts was given the most expansive definition—the humanities, natural science, social sciences, and mathematics. In case you're keeping score, students in business schools had the lowest measurable gains in those critical thinking skills, along with those studying social work, communications, and education.

The study also concluded that liberal arts students finished with the highest measurable gains, in part because those who teach those subjects require more reading and writing than professors in other fields. As far as specialized education is concerned, the Arum study did not challenge the acquisition of critical cognitive skills by students in specialized fields in the context of their chosen specialty, but it did strongly challenge the notion that "field-specific knowledge will inevitably lead to improvement in general skills."[10]

ATTORNEY + RANCHER = GENERALIST

It's 80 degrees in the shade in the backyard of Keith Christian's Los Angeles home. It was the same temperature yesterday and will almost certainly be the same tomorrow, but Keith is really worried about the weather . . . 1,300 miles away.[11] From his laptop he is tracking a heat wave in Kansas. Then, after a quick break to chastise his dog for going into his garden and to listen to his four-year-old daughter's recounting of an exciting day at preschool, he calls a friend in Nebraska to get his take on the lack of rain. Keith has to make a decision because he has 600 head of cattle in eastern Colorado on pastures that desperately need rain.

It's likely that Keith hasn't read "Improving Undergraduate Learning" and has never heard of Liz Coleman. But he, by necessity, ranks as a generalist, if you can define generalist as somebody capable enough to be both a cattleman and an attorney. Keith grew up in the ranch country of Polson, Montana, and rural Hawaii before heading to Yale University and Columbia Law School. He never had a set path, but a man who became his mentor once told Keith to "get the broadest range of experience," so he has tried to do just that.

He spent his summers working on ranches but was also reading constantly. After graduating from Columbia, Keith spent six years working in the mergers and acquisitions department of a big international law firm and once billed 365 hours in 24 days.

He liked the work, but it wasn't working for his life.

Keith is married to the actor Kellie Martin, known for her role as Becca in TV series *Life Goes On* and as the title character in *Christy*, another television series. The two met at Yale. Years later, while Kellie was shooting a film in Montreal, Keith had an epiphany. He was looking after their baby daughter in a hotel room when he realized that this was not how he wanted to spend his time—holed up in a Los Angeles high-rise poring over the tiniest of details on some billion-dollar acquisition deal for a client he would never meet. So he left his firm, although he still does occasional legal work if he has the time and interest—and returned to his ranching roots from the palm tree-lined streets of LA.

"I like doing something different every day and I always have," he said. Ranching by laptop was not exactly how men of his father's generation did the job. Still, he needs to know enough about ranching to talk through problems with his ranch manager from time to time, sometimes daily, if it's calving season. He buys embryos through online auctions and keeps an eye on volatile hay prices from suppliers across the West and Canada. He manages relationships with suppliers and bankers and compliance with government programs.

When he hears that he and his neighboring ranchers are having a hard time getting the fencing and hay feeders they need, he sets up a regional distributorship over the phone and throws just enough of his weight around to get what he and his neighbors need. He is constantly researching and analyzing data on commodity futures, weather, and feed, not to mention the bloodlines of the cows because "the old days of breeding a cow and a bull because you like the looks of 'em are over." He goes to the ranch four to six times a year, working from daybreak to nightfall, and even pitching in on a lot of the hands-on work, like gathering and vaccinating cows. "I need to know a little about a lot of things and know what I am good at and what my ranch manager could do better."[12]

In 2011, Keith's arena of experience expanded once again, this time into retail. He and his wife bought an online toy store, ROMP, (www.rompstore.com) to run collaboratively. Kellie chooses the products, using her experience as a mother and an art history major to curate the store. Keith uses his business experience to manage the back end. They both work out of the house, and "it doesn't feel like work," according to Kellie, with their daughter playing and Keith able to take her swimming at 4 P.M. on a weekday.[13] They have house rules about when work must stop—dinner and bath time.

A hundred and fifty years ago, Keith Christian's approach to life would have been typical. Back then people had to learn to do a lot of different things in a wide variety of fields. Nobody called that being a generalist. It was too common to have a label. But today specialization, for all its gifts and advances, has devalued the person who knows a little about a lot and has valued instead the person who knows a lot about a little.

"The idea of the educated generalist does not exist," said Liz Coleman at an educational summit in 2010, "when breadth is equivalent to shallow and depth is equivalent to the recondite. Until we change that, until we wake up to the fact that education is about the totality of experience . . . we will never break the cycle of failures in this country."[14]

CONFESSIONS OF A GENERALIST

Why such a full-throated defense of generalists in a world where companies are investing billions of dollars in platforms being designed to find, use, and evaluate specialists? In part, because, as technology advances, you still need people greasing the social rails, pulling teams together, driving innovation, and acting as the glue that holds complex undertakings together. As Steve Jobs's biographer Walter Isaacson explained, "Most feats of sustained innovation cannot and do not occur in an iconic garage or the workshop of an ingenious inventor. They occur when people of diverse talents and mind-sets and expertise are brought together, preferably in close physical proximity where they can have frequent meetings and serendipitous encounters."[15]

Welcome to the true confessions portion of the book. It just so happens that your faithful authors are loud and proud generalists. Ryan majored in history, and Jeremy studied English. Neither of us can write an iPhone app, repair a car, or fix a leaky aortic valve—or a radiator, for that matter. But we try to bring value to organizations and to our community by being able to connect people, ideas, and skills. And along the way each of us has built a career and a life that allow us to further the cause of the Smart Generalist. Of course, in a world that still prizes specialists, the road hasn't always been easy, and we've had to rely a good deal on our winning smiles and our boyish charm. But we've learned a thing or two along the way and can offer a bit of hard-won wisdom.

For Ryan, the realization that he could not be a specialist occurred in law school. "As I sat in class and delved deeper and deeper into the substantive areas of law—property, torts, corporate, and criminal—it became clear to me that I didn't want to spend my day thinking about just one area of law. It is not in my nature and not what I would be good at," Ryan explained. "So I knew I had to find another path quickly."

Ryan's path turned out to look more like the Los Angeles freeway system. In a given week Ryan serves in elective office, helps run a start-up, teaches university classes, and does various projects for companies. It suits him: "It's never dull because every day has entirely different challenges. If you add up all the work, it pays the mortgage and allows me to stay interested. There is also some level of job security because I haven't put all my eggs and skills in one basket."

Ryan said it can be difficult to explain his value to potential employers, who are looking to fill an opening and put potential employees in a nice neat HR box. But Ryan never takes no for an answer—he is part politician, after all—and says to employers, "Let's have a conversation. Let's see where the holes in your organization are and see if there is a value I can bring." While others may be unsure, he is confident in his role. "All these positions have different titles, but essentially my job is to be a generalist. When I was mayor, my job wasn't to pave the roads, pick up the trash, or respond to emergency calls. My job was to get those services to the community and take the community's concerns back to the specialists. In many ways I do the same thing in business and teaching."

His advice to those who, like him, can't imagine doing one thing all day long or, heaven forbid, one thing for an entire career, is simple:

My value, like all generalists', is to know a little about a lot. That means the onus is on me to constantly reach out to new people, read books and articles, watch the trends in a wide range of arenas, and generally be passionately interested in the world. Having that broad knowledge to draw on, and to be able to use it when I need it, brings me a lot of credibility when I'm dealing with people in business, government, or academia. I'm always amazed that when I can recall a perfect contact from a conference I was at five years ago or an interesting idea from a *New Yorker* article that I read last month, it can bring value to an organization at the moment they most need it. These little bits of wisdom seemingly had no relevance to my work at the time. But they seem to come in handy just when I need them.

Such broad knowledge—what looks very much like Hirsch's cultural literacy—is the stock-in-trade of the Smart Generalist.

Ironically Jeremy's pathway to becoming a generalist started out with a stint in a highly specialized job. For nine years he flew search-and-rescue helicopters in the US Navy. The demands of that job required thousands of hours of training to become good at a few specialized tasks. "Landing your helicopter on the flight deck of a pitching and rolling ship in the middle of the night takes a lot of skill and precision," Jeremy said. "That's not exactly the time to be thinking big thoughts about the latest economic trends or the political news of the day."

While his job as a navy pilot was exciting and rewarding, Jeremy often found that the hours of training and the constant focus on precision satisfied only half his brain. "Memorizing emergency procedures or learning every mechanical detail of my helicopter were absolutely essential to the job, but that kind of specialized focus could also be pretty mind numbing." To keep a balance, Jeremy tried to find more creative outlets. As an English major in college, he had dabbled in writing short stories. So Jeremy turned to writing as a way to balance the precision and specialization of flying. "When I was in flight school, I actually managed to get a children's bedtime story published. I might be the only navy pilot in history to combine those two talents," he added with a grin.

When Jeremy got out of the navy, he enrolled in a master's program at Harvard's Kennedy School of Government. He was drawn to the Kennedy School's mantra of creating leaders who could easily navigate the intersections of the public, private, and nonprofit sectors; in other words, the Kennedy School seemingly set out to create Smart Generalists. "I was drawn to the idea of solving big, interesting, complex problems and this seemed like a great way to get a broad education to prepare me for that role," Jeremy said.

However, when he got to Harvard, he found a very different reality. "The faculty and staff didn't want to view me as a broad-based problem solver. Instead, because of my military background, I got pigeonholed as a guy who cares only about defense and national security issues. That was really discouraging, and it took a while to break out of that mold." In hindsight Jeremy doesn't find the pigeonholing surprising. "I think people naturally want to classify each other. And we'll do so based on the most readily available information we have about each other." This penchant for classifying each other is a by-product of an economy dominated by Super Specialists. It is manifested in a particularly strong way among human relations professionals, who are constantly trying to hire employees by fitting round pegs into round holes and thus filling openings at their firm. "I wanted to be a square peg," Jeremy said.

In an effort to build his generalist credentials, Jeremy took a job as a management consultant after he graduated from Harvard. Most of his clients were government agencies, including the Federal Emergency Management Agency (FEMA), which was still reeling from its failures in the wake of Hurricane Katrina. "I thought I'd finally have the chance to do some big-picture thinking, to provide advice on how to solve some big, thorny problem. Boy, was I wrong." Instead Jeremy found that the federal government hired consultants less for their strategic advice and more to put butts in seats, treating them more like adjunct employees than big-picture problem solvers.

"Honestly, the only option I saw was to start my own company," Jeremy said. Indeed the skills required to be the CEO of a small growing company are the very definition of a Smart Generalist. "I have to be able to navigate a bunch of different disciplines and deal with a wide variety of stakeholders during the course of the average day. I need to know a little bit about financing, accounting, facilities management, architecture, design, IT networking, security, and, yes, even the janitorial sciences. More important, I need the leadership and communication skills to bring these disparate specialties together into a coherent whole." As the CEO of a coworking company, Jeremy relies on his customers to be his teachers. "At NextSpace, we have close to 1,000 members, all of whom are really good at something, often many things. Having the ability to tap into that collective expertise makes my job easier. In return, I try to offer my skills as a generalist, recognizing big-picture patterns and synthesizing trends, then wrangling people together to solve problems and create value."

In a world built for specialists this isn't always an easy task and one that isn't always recognized as essential. But the dawn of the Age of the Generalist may be upon us. In his groundbreaking 2005 book, *A Whole New Mind: Why Right-Brainers Will Rule the World,* Dan Pink was among the first to recognize the subtle but seismic shift toward favoring generalists. In Pink's analysis many of the specialized tasks that dominated our economy through the end of the twentieth century—things like crunching numbers and cranking out computer code—have been automated or sent offshore. Because of this shift Pink said, "The keys to the kingdom are changing hands. The future belongs to a very different kind of person with a very different kind of mind: creators and empathizers, pattern recognizers, and meaning makers. These people—artists, inventors, designers, storytellers, caregivers, consolers, big-picture think-ers—will now reap society's richest rewards and share its great-est joy."[16] We couldn't agree more.

How will we bridge the gap between specialists and gener-alists? What kind of organizational structures will be required to make this marriage survive and thrive? In Chapter 6 we'll take a look at the new kinds of organizations that are emerging in the Naked Economy to create some marriages and a whole lotta flings between specialists and generalists.

CHAPTER 6

BARELY CORPORATE

Naked Organizations for the Naked Economy

Individual commitment to a group effort—that is what makes a team work, a company work, a society work, a civilization work.

—Vince Lombardi

WHO IS YOUR A-TEAM?

Human extinction is just hours away. Aliens have teamed up with a crazed scientist to develop a weapon that will turn us all into flesh-eating zombies. Our cities will be destroyed by tidal waves and darkness. The militaries of the world and their weapons are useless. Who can save us?

Versions of this scenario are played out on movie screens every summer. More often than not, the heroes who save us from these "end of life as we know it" threats are a ragtag team of ne'er-do-wells, usually the computer geek with a penchant for DNA sequencing, the suave antihero down on his luck, the nerdy yet ridiculously attractive woman with a convenient PhD in astrophysics, and the crazy guy hanging on to his sanity by a thread. Individually these misfits have been cast aside by society. But when the chips are down, when the fate of the entire known universe is uncertain, when the survival of the human race is at stake, this motley crew reassembles as the last best hope for our species.

Why does this plot so appeal to us year after year? Every summer Hollywood bets we will part with our $10 to see how, not if, this ragtag team of heroes saves us. Perhaps we buy the ticket because we all long to be the hero, to be plucked from obscurity because our heretofore underappreciated talents are just what the world needs in its moment of crisis. But we also know that, deep down, neither we nor Batman can do it alone (see Robin, Batgirl, and the butler, Alfred). We need someone to disarm the bomb, shoot the alien when it has us hanging from the ledge of a building, listen to our fears and wry observations just before we plow our plane into the power center of the enemy's ship, and kiss the girl when our plan not only works but somehow we, against all odds, survive.

Work, whether saving the planet from blood-sucking aliens or building a really cool app, is a lot more fun and effective with other people. All the high-tech communication platforms in the world aren't going to change that. The question for the modern organization—everything from two freelancers collaborating on a project to Fortune 500 companies—is how to bring together specialists and generalists in way that allows them the flexibility they want and the interaction they need.

TODAY'S TEAMING

In his book *Free Agent Nation,* Daniel Pink provides a good description of the model for the future of work; although the book came out in 2001, he accurately predicted much of what the economy has become. He used the analogy of the movie industry to discuss how project-based work works. He observed that movies, from blockbusters to art-house films, are created by quickly assembled teams. Actors, grips, directors, extras, and editors join hundreds or even thousands of other professionals on a project-by-project basis. Sometimes they have worked together before, but often they have not. But each plays a role, big or small, until the film is completed. The team then disassembles. The film is a success or failure, and the players find new teams for their next project.[1]

This project-oriented future of the workplace is going to demand skilled managers (or producers, in Pink's example, and Smart Generalists in our lexicon) and well-designed organizations, just as the traditional workplace has. Someone must organize the players for a common purpose. Just as workers have to adapt to new demands of the Naked Economy, managers will as well.

Team building has been a corporate cliché for at least 20 years, but too often it was used to describe instilling values of forced participation in a group of people who had already been assembled, if you can call a full-time staff in a traditional office setting a team. In a work world based on the Hollywood model of project-directed tasks, "team building" is a phrase used more literally. When faced with a certain task or project, a manager will typically start by assembling a team from scratch to fit the demands of the job.

Harvard Business School professor Amy Edmondson uses a compelling basketball analogy to describe this dynamic, which is increasingly common in the work world. She says that project-based work is more like a pick-up basketball game than a game in an organized league in which players have been teammates for years. It is, she says, management on the fly. In an April 2012 piece in the *Harvard Business Review,* Edmondson coined the term *teaming* (which she has since used as the title for an excellent book) to describe the emerging practice of assembling teams of professionals to perform a given job. Managers in a traditional workplace must work with the skill sets they have available on staff, and their ability to address tasks as they come up is often limited by the flexibility and versatility of their staff. Instead, a Smart Generalist works as a project leader to assemble a team of individuals for a specific task; what Smart Generalists can deliver is limited only by their contact list.

As the nature of project-based work becomes more technologically complex, and as the skills required to complete the work become increasingly diverse, team builders need to be nimble and creative in how they assemble, dis-assemble, then re-assemble the talent they need. Edmondson points to another vivid analogy by way of illustration: "Think of clinicians in an emergency room, who convene quickly to solve a specific patient problem and then move on to address other cases with different colleagues, compared with the surgical team that performs the same procedure under highly controlled conditions day after day."[2]

When crisis is the norm and the challenges we face are not predictable, the ragtag misfits really may be those who are called upon more often to save the world. After all, no single established team can prepare for the asymmetrical threats of aliens, mad scientists, tidal waves, and credit default swaps. No one individual, or any specific group of individuals, is brilliant enough to solve such a wide variety of problems. Each problem demands a customized set of minds and talents—our Super Specialists—to deal with it.

The manager's job, like the Hollywood producer's, can be a daunting task of organization. The first step is to get an accurate read of the project at hand, determining what kinds of skills and expertise are needed and recruiting those individuals best suited for the job. As Edmondson's article discusses, in a global marketplace for talent, cultural differences have to be anticipated and transcended.

A physical example of this process is the design and construction of the enormous Water Cube, the beautiful blue bubble-wrapped aquatic center at the 2008 Beijing Olympic Games.[3] It was built on a tight deadline and budget, using an array of 20 international firms collaborating across continents, languages, expertise, and cultures.

The Water Cube is a 340,000-square-foot rectangular box that held as many as 17,000 spectators and was under the microscope of every news organization in the world. The structure is covered in an ethereal, semitransparent polymer that was invented in Japan, designed by Australians, built by the Chinese, and approved by the International Olympic Committee. As a design spectacle, the Water Cube is a wonder, winning all kinds of design and engineering awards and costing more than 10 billion yuan—about US$1.6 billion. Several big companies were brought in, including the China State Construction Engineering Corporation, China Construction Design International, and the London-based multinational corporation Arup.

The engineers of Arup faced the daunting task of bridging considerable cultural differences, not just ethnicity and nationality but also corporate and occupational differences. Arup's first step was to engage local experts and partners in extensive contract negotiations that tried to anticipate any and all issues that might arise. According to the Association for Project Management, which gave Arup its Project of the Year Award for the Water Cube, "At the implementation plan workshop, Arup's project management team focused initially on the need to articulate and communicate a very clear project vision for the Water Cube design. This was intended to have multiple benefits. Most simply, the vision would provide improved clarity and autonomy to the design team members. This would help achieve a quality outcome in a very short period of time, by allowing parallel streams of activity to converge quickly and accurately. It was also hoped that having a robust vision would greatly help achieve alignment and buy-in from other project stakeholders."[4]

Once a project has been sized up, the team leader must provide some kind of structure in which the recruited experts can operate, get to know each other, and figure out the most efficient and mutually satisfying ways to communicate and provide feedback. New communication technologies can make this possible on a global scale. For example, for the Water Cube project, Arup created four distinct teams with specific tasks, which divided component parts of the Water Cube into discrete projects, instituted daily communication and briefings by these teams, and provided on-the-ground management.

Even with excellent planning, cultural differences and the inevitable personality clashes will be a barrier to smooth collaboration. Leaders in the new economy are going to feel the pressure to anticipate those differences for the sake of the project. As the project-oriented work model becomes more common, certain cultural and interpersonal protocols will become established. But managers are still going to have the find the right mix of personalities to meet their deadlines.

A team of researchers, Ella Miron-Spektor, Miriam Erez, and Eitan Naveh, studied more than 40 research-and-development teams at a major defense contractor and found their members had three major cognitive working styles: creative, detail oriented, and conformist.

The creatives, as the name implies, are the idea people. They tend to be experimental, what-if, outside-the-box thinkers but are often impatient with rules and procedure and are not always practical or collaborative. Detail-oriented people can be counted on to get the numbers right but are often risk averse. Conformists play the key role of implementing what the creatives come up with, following corporate policies and culture by the book. About half of workers, the study found, represent a mix of different work styles.

The researchers found that a successful project team has an ideal ratio of each worker type, and conformists make up a big part of that. The most successful innovative teams had about 10 percent detail-oriented folks, 20 to 30 percent creative types, and 10 to 20 percent conformists. The remaining members of the team had mixed work styles. Short of requiring workers to wear badges declaring their work style, leaders have to develop methods to identify these styles in anyone they might be considering for a project.

The upshot of the research was counterintuitive: as important as detail-oriented people are, the more successful teams tended to have more conformists or, to quote the Miron-Specktor study itself, "conformists, though they may be useless at generating breakthrough ideas, dramatically increase a team's radical innovations" by actually making the innovations happen within the context of real life.[5]

COLLABORATING CROWDS

As that horrifying old cliché goes, there is more than one way to skin a cat, and in the department of cat skinning, InnoCentive certainly qualifies as innovative. InnoCentive is a pioneer in crowd-sourcing solutions to business problems.[6] And it does it in a way that suggests it might be a lot of fun for everyone involved. It is called "Challenge Driven Innovation," which essentially means it's a contest.

InnoCentive was created by Alpheus Bingham and Aaron Schach, who, while working for the pharmaceutical giant Eli Lilly, thought there had to be a better way to do research and development. They raised money, hired a team, and opened for business in 2001, to serve various corporate, government and nonprofit clients who are looking for solutions to specific problems in the field of innovation, usually involving science and technology. In turn, the New England–based company will reposition the particular problem as a Challenge, which it then presents to its 260,000 Solvers from almost 200 countries for a cash award, the highest of which reached $1 million.

On its website, InnoCentive makes a pitch to Solvers that appeals to the intellectual challenge of taking on a particularly difficult puzzle: "Forget Sudoku, Challenges are real problems requiring sustained concentration, critical thinking, research, creativity, and synthesis of knowledge. Developing a solution is incredibly rewarding and an unparalleled mental workout."

Once registered, a Solver becomes part of the Global Solver Community and can scan the various Challenges for anything that matches the Solver's interests and specialist skill set. The company has posted more than 1,400 Challenges from various corporate entities and agencies and has given out more than 1,200 awards totaling more than $35 million. More than 60 percent of the Solver community has advanced degrees.

Among those who have won Challenge awards are:

Ben Skowera, a Pennsylvania software developer who won the *Economist*-InnoCentive Transparency Challenge by applying the same metrics used in online dating and social media sites to delivering easily digestible political analysis.

New Zealand's Russell McMahon, an electrical engineer who came up with a solar-powered flashlight that provides families in developing countries with reliable and affordable nighttime ambient light.

Engineers Without Borders, a group from the University of Washington that created a device that disinfects water using the sun's rays.

Typical of InnoCentive's competitions is a 2012 initiative by the *Economist*, the British newsweekly. The *Economist* was looking to create graphics from the mountain of data it was getting from the Nielsen Corporation about consumer behavior. It brought in InnoCentive to challenge its army of Solvers to design a compelling infographic.

For companies, InnoCentive provides a vast resource of potential talent not necessarily in the market to contract for project-based work but who might take up the challenge of solving a particularly thorny technological problem. The

Solvers often find new approaches to issues that, for whatever reason, had stymied internal specialists on payroll.

The InnoCentive approach was even applied to the most infamous technological predicament of recent years, the Deepwater Horizon oil spill—aka the BP oil spill—of 2010. InnoCentive issued the Challenge to its Solver community to help figure out a workable method BP could use to stop oil from pouring into the Gulf of Mexico. It was the first Challenge posted on InnoCentive with no cash award.

The problem attracted more than 900 complex but promising technological solutions, but BP was not interested in any of them. InnoCentive's CEO, Dwayne Spradlin, said that although it would have cost BP nothing to at least consider the proposals the Solvers offered for Deepwater Horizon, the British oil giant declined the offer of help.[7]

BP's refusal is a frustrating example of what happens when innovative thinking and new ways of organizing talent clash with the old top-down model of doing business. But, on the hopeful side, InnoCentive's Challenge provides a model for how crowd-sourcing technology could be deployed during a national or international emergency. Remember, we might need to find misfits to save us from an alien attack someday.

A 2009 study commissioned by InnoCentive examined its economic impact on one client company, the Swiss agribusiness Syngenta, which engaged InnoCentive to run 56 Challenges during a three-year period. Syngenta estimated that its cost for conceiving of and evaluating each Challenge was about $10,000, and the awards paid out for successful solutions was just under $1.9 million, for a total expense of about $2.5 million.

Compare that to Syngenta's estimate that it would have had to pay $120,000 per scientist per project, assuming that each project needed only one specialist. At that rate the 56 projects would have cost the company more than $6.7 million in salary alone. Syngenta also estimated its savings in time, figuring it saved about 480 person-hours by using InnoCentive's Challenge system.[8]

InnoCentive represents an emerging trend in large-scale problem solving known as "swarm work" that, at least theoretically, could bring to bear the expertise of the entire world to solve a single business problem. This approach is what Spradlin calls the "new normal." "We've got organizations that need to figure out how to make talent and work pools function globally. Organizations need to figure out a way to move from fixed procedures and infrastructure to variable ones in organizing and optimizing resources. We've got the millennial generation coming in, and if anything, they're more project-based, not jobs-based, which means we need to think about how to orchestrate work talent in an environment of constant churn. There is a need for a whole new business science that can help organizations function more effectively," said Spradlin in an Aspen Institute study called "The Future of Work."[9]

ORGANIZATIONS BY THE PEOPLE, FOR THE PEOPLE

From the standpoint of commercial and government clients, the InnoCentive approach appears to be both efficient and cost effective, at least when it comes to certain problems that have always defied internal analysis. But from the worker's point of view, introducing project-to-project competitions, while potentially rewarding, doesn't necessarily make for a stable or reliable income. In that respect, the InnoCentive model works best for those already in some kind of salaried position or with another source of income.

The challenge for project-based platforms, whether they offer participants millions like InnoCentive or pennies like Mechanical Turk, is creating a sustainable living for their users. Jonathan Zittrain, director of the Berkman Center for the Internet and Society at Harvard, has pointed out that they might be creating "digital sweatshops." Pay on these platforms will "reflect intense competition within a huge labor pool," which drives down wages, particularly as workers from less developed nations come online and are willing to work for considerably less than their peers in wealthier countries. Zittrain also notes that "online contracting circumvents a range of labor laws and practices, found in most developed countries, that govern worker protections, minimum wage, health and retirement benefits, child labor, and so forth."[10]

This is where Sara Horowitz and the Freelancers Union come into play. The Freelancers Union has been working tirelessly for more than a decade to organize independent workers and create a new safety net. Horowitz calls for a "new mutualism"—a movement that relies on sustainable, community-driven solutions to seemingly intractable problems. The Freelancers Union organizes independent workers to have a voice in the political system as well as harness the power of numbers to get health insurance, retirement plans, and employment protections.

Horowitz correctly notes that "mutual support is nothing new. The first wave of mutualism saw the spread of worker and farmer cooperatives, credit associations, friendly societies, and similar groups. The government-sponsored programs of the New Deal supplanted the need for many of these groups, but as government- and business-sponsored supports are dwindling, interest in mutualism is growing, and advances in technology make it easier for communities to stay connected."[11]

If workers can use these networks, organizing in the new economy will not be left to solely those with capital or a corporate designation. It will be incumbent on workers to form networks and organizations so they can leverage their talent and time. This will benefit management and the workforce as well as the overall economy. Tammy Johns, a senior vice president for the famous temp agency Manpower, told the Aspen Institute working group on the future of work that creating these organizations carries a certain urgency. Johns indicated that work responsibilities are becoming more complex and socialized, the boundaries between work and personal life are blurring, and the shift from manufacturing to services is putting a greater premium on people's ability to solve complex problems and show sophisticated judgment. To succeed, both individual workers and companies will have to move quickly and adapt to the dictates of changing circumstances.

MANAGING ON A CLOUD

Nearly 40 percent of US workers could do at least some parts of their jobs by working from home. Although about 3 out of 4 employers say that they trust employees working from home to do their work, about a third of those employers would prefer to have some means to monitor employees who are working from home.

This mindset is perfectly exemplified by Yahoo! CEO Marissa Mayer's now famous March 2013 edict that required all employees to work at the office. The policy touched off an international debate about flexibility in the modern work-place and drew scorching criticism from working parents and others interested in a more flexible work arrangement. One Ya-hoo employee called it "outrageous and a morale killer."[12] The impact of Mayer's policy is yet to be known both in terms of increased innovation (her stated reason for the change) and Yahoo's ability to attract and retain the best and the brightest in the field.

Other companies, however, put enormous faith in a disag-gregated workforce model, where workers are spread across a wide range of workplaces (more on this in Chapter 8) instead of aggregated into big office buildings and corporate campuses. "I would argue that most offices are full of people not work-ing," said Matthew Mullenweg, founder and president of the San Francisco–based start-up Automattic. "At least if they're working from home, they don't have to pretend like they're working."[13]

Matt is something of a star in the software development world, thanks to his primary invention and Automattic's most prominent property, the popular open-source blogging ar-chitecture WordPress. Automattic also produces the Akismet antispam tool, the Ping-O-Matic pinging software, and the so-cial networking plug-in Buddy Press, among others.[14] Matt is a true believer in the officeless future. He calls the traditional office itself a distraction. "It's the arbitrary colocation of a num-ber of adults for no apparent reason. Who's sitting where, who brought the funny-smelling lunch, who's talking on the phone too loudly, the old computers, the whole environment. It's just not very creative," he said.[15]

When Automattic was founded in 2005, its first partners were transatlantic: in the United Kingdom (Great Britain and Northern Ireland), Ireland, and the United States (Texas and

California). On its website, Automattic provides an interactive map showing all its employees around the world. They are concentrated in the United States and Europe, but Africa, Asia, and South America are also represented. A closer look shows that diversity lies not only in its internationality but in the types of places its employees call home: rural and urban, tech hubs and less developed countries.

Using this disaggregated workforce model, WordPress has fast become one of the world's most popular and durable software products. By the fall of 2012, the web had more than 56 million WordPress sites. More than 364 million people view more than 2.5 billion pages each month. The average day brings about half a million new posts from users and about 400,000 comments to those posts. Among the most high-profile WordPress users are the *New York Times,* CNN, eBay, General Motors, and any number of teenage rock stars and/or boy bands.

Matt's experience with a distributed workforce has made him militant when it comes to traditional office space. "Even for those who are creative, just by the virtue of having a location where they have to be, you encourage all kinds of unproductive behavior, like getting there early before the boss and leaving late, after the boss, or staying awake all day. If you're tired, and you need a nap, take a nap. You will come back to work far more refreshed and creatively charged than if you were dazed for the rest of the afternoon."

Automattic now employs about 120 people all over the world. Two-thirds of its workers are based in the United States; the remainder lives in 90 cities in 24 countries. "We can hire the best people regardless of geographical location," Matt said.

Just as the guiding principle of InnoCentive is to unleash the world's brainpower on specific business challenges, Matt and Automattic are true believers in breaking the bonds of geography in staffing a company. "It opens up the pool of available talent, which is always a good thing. So why not open it up to the seven billion people in the world?"

Matt spends his time in San Francisco, New York, and Houston (his hometown). When Automattic's leaders got together for a board meeting in San Francisco, they designed a work space called the Lounge in a former restaurant. Its sole purpose is to provide a space for human interaction. Thus Automattic might be the first tech company to have a techless headquarters. "There were just a bunch of couches and tables. No computers anywhere," Matt noted proudly.

For the Automattic employee, the ability to work anywhere is the ability to "arbitrage your quality of life," as Matt put it. He points to workers who've moved to dream locales from Europe to Southeast Asia. Just before we interviewed him, one of WordPress's editors announced to Matt that she was moving to Vietnam for "a couple of months." It was not a request, rather a statement, and her assignment would continue unchanged. "I have a colleague who came to me and said, 'There are two places in the country I want to live.' One was Tybee Island, Georgia. And the other was Santa Cruz. She chose Tybee Island." Yet another employee traveled around the world for a year, working and documenting his experience on, you guessed it, a WordPress site.

However, lest you think that the distributed model is simply a way of reducing costs or stems from a belief that technology has made the office irrelevant, Matt's management strategy is based on human interaction. "It's never been a cost thing for us," he said. "Because once you end up flying people around all over the place, it ends up costing about the same as the office would cost to begin with." And, boy, do they fly people all over the place. Teams decide quarterly where they want to meet, and Automattic flies them there—Iceland, Australia, Europe, or Asia. What matters is not the place but what happens once the Automattic employees get there. Matt said he's a believer in face-to-face interaction: "There is nothing more valuable in companies such as this one than collaborative brainstorming with five or ten people. And that's just easier to do in person, and there is some intense fun-having that goes with that as well. We make an effort to hang out. I mean, we'll have one person in Berlin, another in Reykjavik, Iceland. But we'll come together somewhere. I was on the road 245 days last year, and a big chunk of that was working."

Automattic works hard to connect its global teams in other ways, too. The company requires its employees to give "flash talks," TED-style lectures to their colleagues on any subject that might strike their fancy. "There have been racy ones. Sometimes people just show pictures of their kids or talk about their hobbies," Matt said. "Some people advocate for change in the company. Anything goes." Also part of the culture is something called "hack weeks," when teams are established to tinker intensely on a nagging problem. The teams are always mixed up, so that no one gets comfortable with a fixed set of people.

"I think the important principle for us is to make sure everyone is on an even footing with everyone else. So it's important to have these kinds of conversations where each person is equally part of it. That's the key."[16]

YOUR COMPANY FLASHES SOME LEG

Not yet ready to turn your company's business plan into InnoCentive Challenges or have your office manager work from Vietnam? It's OK. This is a process in which the rules are being made up as we go. But Jeanne Meister, former chief learning officer at Sun Microsystems and coauthor of *WorkPlace 2020*, thinks you ignore these shifts at your peril: "The next decade will usher in new companies and business models that are unimaginable today and will dramatically change how we live, work, learn, communicate and play. Anticipating these changes will be critical to your ability to thrive in the 2020 workplace, where transparency, collaboration, personalization, and hyper connectivity will rule the day."[17]

PART III

WI-FI, WORK, AND WATER COOLERS

*How Work Is Changing
but People Are Not*

CHAPTER 7

PEOPLE

Putting the Humans Back in Human Resources

It has become appallingly obvious that our technology has exceeded our humanity.

—Albert Einstein

BIKES, BEER, AND A BETTER BUSINESS STRATEGY

Bicycling and beer are generally not thought of as particularly complementary activities. Usually, if you do one, you should avoid the other.

But bikes and beer are deeply entwined at New Belgium Brewing—and not only because of the recognizable bike-centered logo of its flagship product, Fat Tire Amber Ale. The bicycle, in fact, is a symbol of what makes New Belgium such a desirable place to work and a model company for the Naked Economy.

According to the American craft-beer maker's creation story, the idea to start the company came to cofounder Jeff Lebesch during a bike trip across Belgium in 1988. In a video in which Lebesch explains New Belgium's founding, his bike is mounted to a wall behind him with an arrow pointing to a worn bicycle seat. The arrow is emblazoned with the proclamation: "We were conceived here."[1]

New Belgium keeps that connection alive with its rank and file through a whimsical—and very popular—program of perks. At every employee's first anniversary with the company, he or she is awarded a brand new cruiser-style bicycle which is specially designed for that year. Thus, at New Belgium's twin facilities in Fort Collins, Colorado and Asheville, North Carolina an employee's seniority is illustrated by the model year of the bicycle that he or she rides to work.

At five years, that same employee is given an all-expenses-paid trip to recreate the bike tour that inspired the company's founding. Belgium, as any beer snob can tell you, is to hand-crafted beer what Kona, Hawaii is to coffee. It is in Belgium where beers made at Trappist monasteries became beloved by beer drinkers worldwide, spurring the epicurean market for craft beers in which New Belgium competes today.

Free bicycles and trips to Europe—not to mention a complimentary 12-pack every week—are certainly enough to get the attention of talented young people looking for a career landing spot, but if that were all New Belgium offered, the brewery would be merely a market curiosity. Indeed, the perks keep coming for long-term employees—at 10 years, you qualify for a 4–6 week paid sabbatical. These perks, along with full health benefits and paid time off, have repeatedly garnered recognition from Outside Magazine and others who have declared New Belgium to be in the top 30 "Best Places to Work" for three successive years.[2]

While these awards are impressive, New Belgium is not satisfied with merely being, "employee friendly." CEO Kim Jordan declared, "At New Belgium, we believe passionately that our culture and employees are our strategic differentiators. That is why we commit the amount of time and resources in remaining culturally connected as our company continues to prosper and grow in size and geography."[3] Culturally connected not only means perks, but also democratic governance. New Belgium practices "open-book management" meaning that all employees have access to the company's financials. Recognizing that transparency doesn't mean a lot without knowledge, employees are trained in how to read financial documents, attend monthly all-staff meetings where questions are answered, and are provided with online dashboard metrics so that progress is monitored and even more questions can be asked.[4]

Recently, that ethos pushed the company to take its vision to the next level by becoming employee-owned through an Employee Stock Option Plan (ESOP). Each of its more than 450 workers now has an ownership stake and a say in the company's decision-making. At the beginning of 2013, New Belgium went from a 41-percent employee-owned status to 100 percent. After 1,000 hours on the job, New Belgium employees go through an ownership ceremony in which newly vested workers are given a token of their new ownership stake and are asked to stand before the crowd at a company-wide staff meeting and express their hopes and desires for the company.

Bryan Simpson came to New Belgium back in 1997, only six years after the company's founding. A graduate of Colorado State University in Fort Collins and veteran broadcast journalist, he had worked for four different television stations over the course of seven or eight years.

"When I came back to my college town, I had a couple of buddies who were telling me, 'Yeah, you should check this

out,'" said Bryan who is now New Belgium's community relations director.[5] "It was a very small craft brewer at that point
with only 55 people working there. I decided to work there just
for the summer and have some fun with it, but I immediately
fell in love with the culture there. I would be in the hallway and
two people would be having high-level discussions about engineering challenges or philosophies. All kinds of people from
different backgrounds were working here and I just found that
I was super engaged every day, and it was exciting to me, and I
thought this could be for the long haul."

New Belgium cultivates an ownership mentality among its
employees not only through stock, but by recruiting workers to
join various governance committees on topics such as sustainability, philanthropy, health and wellness, and others. These
committees composed of people at all levels and professional
backgrounds devise policies that they then have to sell to fellow committees and the executive team. The company's CEO
and co-founder Jordan sits atop a hierarchy that also includes
an internal board of directors known as the Compass Management Team. The committees and Compass Management Team
have tremendous authority to set the strategy and tactics for
New Belgium, which has seen its revenues grow more than 15
percent a year to more than $140 million in 2012.[6]

"It's a very flat-feeling organization," Bryan observes, "in
the sense that there's a lot of lateral communications and people are talking back and forth across these strata."

The coolness factor of working at New Belgium is off the
charts, considering not only the bikes and the trips to Belgium,
but the work environment which includes everything from
working in a green building, yoga classes, foosball tables, and
cyclo-cross biking on the campus. Fort Collins and Asheville are

also extremely attractive locales for the kind of demographic that values bicycles, hand-crafted beers, and sustainability.

But the real innovation at New Belgium brewing is its insistence on maintaining a genuinely democratic work environment on the notion that workers fully invested in the company's success are going to be happy, productive, and committed. The company's 93 percent employee-retention rate and remarkable growth from beer making in a basement to the second largest distributor of hand-crafted beers in the United States in a little more than two decades speaks to the success of the plan.

HUMANS AS RENEWABLE RESOURCE

As we continue to move further away from the industrial and information economies of the last century and toward the innovation economy of this century, it's worth figuring out what motivates people to be creative, innovative, and collaborative.

Indeed, the view that talented people are a resource worth cultivating and worth renewing is an enormous leap forward. For most of the history of human work, "human resource management" meant thinking of employees the same way that we think of any other natural resource, like oil, timber, minerals, or land. Human resources were merely another input in the business process, something to be managed, maximized, and often discarded when the process was complete. Even though our economy and our society have come a long way since, say, the sweatshop factories of the nineteenth century, many companies still measure people by their productive output without giving much thought to what it takes to sustain that output. We know more about how to maximize the output of an internal combustion engine than we do about how to maximize and sustain the output of the creative individuals who now form the base of our innovation economy. So, there's a growing sense that a management and motivation approach that resembles New Belgium's is indeed the wave of the future.

Things are not always rosy at New Belgium. About a decade into its existence, the company endured a round of layoffs that shook the employees' confidence in their carefully crafted democratic work culture.

"We had hired up for engineering jobs and then the work dried up as we went through a different phase," remembered Bryan. "The layoffs came down as a surprise to everyone and if you want to talk about a tear in the culture, this was a pretty big one."

Soon, there were whispers in the hallways that the layoffs meant a departure from the New Belgium way of doing business. Everything felt different. The vibe was not healthy.

CEO Jordan brought her employees together and began a dialogue on what had happened and what had gone wrong.

"She took questions for four hours one day," said Bryan, "and the next day we all sat down again for another four hours. So when it comes to pushback, people can get pretty serious about that too. The end result is if you have a healthy, respectful process, then people are going to support that, whether or not their decision was the decision that won the day."

MEET YOUR NEW COWORKERS

New Belgium's holistic management style may be well suited to the new rules of work that are being written by the millennial generation, those 88 million souls born between 1977 and 1997 who will soon dominate the workforce and who are putting enormous bottom-up pressure on the how, where, and why of work. A 2010 Harvard Business Review study found that millennials see work as an integral part of their lives, as opposed to a necessary evil that must be balanced by other, more fulfilling, activities, an attitude common in the boomer generation.

As we noted earlier, millennials have already come to terms with not getting lifetime employment, generous pension and health-care benefits, and Social Security checks that will allow them a measure of security in their golden years. But that doesn't mean they are entering the workforce with no expectations of their employers. This is the generation that, for good or ill, has been subject to helicopter parenting since birth, got a trophy and a blue ribbon for their every activity as kids, and has been polishing their resumés since kindergarten. While these stereotypes are a bit overused and don't universally apply, demographic pressures mean that millennials will face stiff competition in college admissions, even stiffer competition in the job market, and will even have to compete for suitable mates. In many ways millennials have no choice to but to be overachievers. That they've embraced this reality means that millennials are potentially great employees.

But the Harvard study found that millennials' high standards don't apply only to themselves. Millennials also apply them to the companies they want to work for. And one thing they especially expect from their employers is the opportunity to be mentored. At first blush, this desire for mentorship may seem simple and even ancillary, one of those freebies that companies dole out just to make their employees happy. But for the millennials mentoring takes on a much more integral purpose. They see mentoring not just as an opportunity to learn requisite skills; they see it as a chance to become indoctrinated into the culture of a company, to have a sense of the secret sauce that makes the company tick. Most important, they see mentoring as a way for the company to make a personal investment in them, to provide meaning and context to their work, and ultimately to give them a sense of pride and ownership in the company. This sense of pride and ownership puts people at the center of the company, allows workers to see themselves as more than just cogs in a machine, and is an important tool for maximizing and sustaining human productivity.

Mentoring has, of course, been a central part of the work experience since the first Cro-Magnon showed his younger brother how to skin a mammoth. Traditionally mentoring was a way to maintain continuity in a company, but it has also perpetuated a hierarchical corporate structure in which the high-status "old hands" show the ropes to the green kids. But one hallmark of the new workplace and the millennial generation is the penchant for questioning everything, including those hierarchies. So while younger workers very much want mentoring, they may not want it in the traditional manner.

As a result, new ways of mentoring are beginning to emerge. "Reverse mentoring," for example, pairs off new employees with older, more seasoned, ones. But instead of the older employees' holding court, telling the new kids how it's done, the flow of knowledge and information goes the other way. In this model it's the 25-year-old who helps the 45-year-old navigate things like social media and mobile apps. In fact mentoring the upper-level suits in how to use Twitter and an iPhone has important secondary benefits. It allows increased exposure to the boss and provides new hires with a window into how a company works and who holds the decision-making power. This glimpse into the inner workings of the company increases new hires' sense of pride and ownership in the company. On the flip side reverse mentoring exposes the boss to how her employees think, what tools they use, and how they make decisions. It can also make the boss more open to demands for remote working and flex time. This breakdown of traditional hierarchies further serves to put people, rather than rigid corporate structures, back at the center of work.

PEERING ONLY SOUNDS DIRTY

Another twist on mentoring that ignores traditional hierarchies is peer-to-peer mentoring. Peer-to-peer mentoring recognizes two important facts about companies in the new economy. First, it serves to further break down rigid hierarchical corporate structures. Information and directives no longer flow from the top down, but travel horizontally as peers find the best source of information and expertise among themselves rather than from on high. Second, illustrative of the specialist/generalist model that we laid out earlier in the book, peer-to-peer mentoring recognizes that expertise is everywhere within a company and having a tool to discover, unlock, and use that expertise makes people more efficient and effective at their jobs. For example, the British telecommunications company BT instituted a program called Dare2Share, which set up a series of short podcasts and discussion threads to allow workers to share their knowledge with their peers. The program came about after the company found that more than three-quarters of its employees preferred to learn in a peer-to-peer setting and often informally sought the advice and expertise of their peers, rather than looking to the corporate structure to provide answers and direction.

If coworkers can mentor each other with little or no assistance from the higher-ups, why can't they do even more for each other in order to maximize and sustain their productivity? That's the tantalizing question that comes out of the work of Philip Rosedale, known throughout the tech world as the founder of the popular virtual world application Second Life, a creation of his former company, Linden Lab. Philip's new venture is called Coffee & Power, and it is designed to explore just how far peer-to-peer support can go in maximizing and sustaining human productivity in the workplace. It is, of course, a delicious irony that the man who developed the world's most famous virtual environment in which people could interact with each other entirely independent of geography has turned his interests toward making real-world physical proximity and interaction the next killer app.

Coffee & Power operates out of small café-like coworking spaces in San Francisco, Santa Monica, and Portland, Oregon. The spaces work as a kind of marketplace for tech services. Coffee & Power seeks to use the physical nearness of the coworking spaces as an asset through a virtual communications platform that allows coworkers to address those working around them in order to find work or find help. "It's this really interesting app that is designed to facilitate a more structured kind of sharing and interaction between people who happen to be sitting in the same spaces," Philip said. It's a useful piece of technology that definitely draws from Philip's experience with the virtual world of Second Life. But the technology succeeds only by putting people, and their need for community and physical interaction, first.

Even more interesting is how Philip thinks about the reward and feedback mechanisms that can be built into such a

peer-to-peer system. By putting people and their collaborative interactions at the center of the system, then creating a
way to see and understand the value of those collaborations,
Philip believes that his technology can have revolutionary
consequences inside the context of a large established company. The problem, in Philip's estimation, is that companies
are not particularly good at providing feedback to employees
and recognizing them for a job well done. In most companies
performance appraisals flow from the top down through rigid
communications channels. But if you really want to know how
good or bad people are at their jobs, don't ask the boss, ask
their peers.

To address this problem, Philip and his colleagues at Linden Lab developed something called the Love Machine. It's a
peer-to-peer communication platform that offers praise and
gratitude. "You could recognize somebody for a specific task
that they had done inside the company any time you wanted
to, as often as you wanted to," Philip explained. "You had to
identify the other person, and you had to type a Twitter-sized
one-sentence description of what they did. That showed up on
screens all around the office, and it was captured as part of the
recognized person's permanent performance history." The program was meant for positive feedback and praise only.[7]

"It was meant for simple, specific, granular recognition for
jobs well done," Philip continued. "And Love Machine worked
super-well. We made it a material part of your performance review. You'd get to go through all that love you got from other
people, pick out your favorite ten statements every quarter,
and then write a little editorial around why that love was, in
your opinion, reflective of your performance." Linden Lab even
tweaked Love Machine to gain a sense of how the company

itself was performing. The company did a content analysis of the words being used in the Love Machine messages and developed them into a word-frequency cloud. "That gave us a dashboard of what the company was doing or not doing to succeed or fail," Philip said. Tellingly, that dashboard didn't rely on traditional metrics like sales or profits but on what people thought about how well their coworkers were doing their jobs.

The folks at Linden Lab learned a few things as Love Machine evolved and progressed. Philip had heard the skeptics say that such a system would be only a popularity contest. "Actually, it was the opposite," he said. "If anything, it tends to recognize selfless work or hazardous work or tough work that had to get done. It really effectively recognized the people doing the basic blocking and tackling of keeping the company running. If you want to recognize the people who are coming up with the big ideas, the Love Machine isn't so good at that."[8] But by putting people first, breaking down communication and management hierarchies, and relying on peer-to-peer interaction to understand what's really happening in a company, the Love Machine stands as a great example of how to reward and motivate people in the new economy.

TURNING LOVE INTO CASH

The initial success of the Love Machine gave Philip and his colleagues at Linden Lab a tantalizing idea: if the Love Machine was so good at capturing what was actually going on in the workplace by putting people instead of hierarchies at the center of the process, why not take the next logical step in the evolution of the concept? Use Love Machine to determine how much people get paid for their work. Philip is convinced this idea will have profound consequences for the authoritarian hierarchy of the workplace.

Here's what he and his colleagues did: Every quarter the company set aside a pot of money for employees to distribute to their peers. A software program was developed to allow these transactions to take place anonymously over two days. The short time window minimized the opportunity to game the system. "We didn't want people to cooperate," Philip said. "We wanted to keep conversations about it to a minimum and give people less time to think about the process. Following up on the success of Love Machine, we said, 'OK, everybody's sending all this love to their peers. Everybody has this very high degree of peripheral awareness of what everybody else is doing. Now let's send money instead of love. Let's allow people to allocate money anonymously to anybody they want in the company, using any justification that makes sense to them.'"[9]

To seed the project the company put about $300,000 in a pool and gave each employee $1,000 to give out to peers they felt were doing good work. "I strongly believe that this is going to be the dominant mechanism for compensation going forward in the future of work," Philip said.

Arguing against the effectiveness of this system is insane. The idea of using a small set of managers to hand out bonuses, the way it's always been done, just doesn't hold anymore. The difference in quality between that system and this process is really striking in so many ways. With the Love Machine process, bonuses can be handed out frequently, which is wonderful. The process doesn't create the political stress for managers who might inadvertently over- or under-reward someone. That's just a bad idea. And most importantly, it gets everybody's brain involved in evaluating performance. You have a much larger collective mind setting bonuses, so the accuracy of correctly rewarding performance goes way up. And, on top of everything else, consider the cultural strength of an organization that entrusts all of its people to make those kinds of decisions.

Of course the workplace has always been resistant to any kind of democratic impulse. Lest he be accused to fostering a kind of French Revolution in the workplace, Philip said absolute democracy in a company is a bad idea. But in some arenas, opening up the decision-making process makes the most sense for the overall good of the company. "This is really a critically important note about the future of work. What I've described here is not democracy. It's actually a marketplace. That's an important point. Companies—especially small start-up companies—should not be democracies because democracies are often unable to make the kind of bold, sweeping changes that need to happen in a business. And if you're in a situation where you need to make a major destructive change to your strategy, democratic or socialist systems of government are not effective."[10] So Philip agrees that managers are still vital members of an organization. But by relieving managers of the burdens of performance evaluations and using a peer-to-peer system to give that function back to the people who can best make those evaluations, managers get to focus more of their energy and intellect on their core function of growing and strengthening the company. This rethinking of the place that people occupy in an organization—seeing people not as another input to a business process but as an integral, vital part of the process itself—is an instructive example of how questioning everything about the nature of work can lead to greater productivity.

GIVING UP CONTROL

Other evidence suggests that moving away from a rigid corporate hierarchy and adopting more open, collaborative methods can benefit companies in the new economy. In 2007 the consulting and services firm CSC Germany clamped down and exerted more control over its employees and their work in an effort to reverse a decline in the company's revenues. The decision only exacerbated the problem. Later, however, CSC took the opposite tack and initiated an experiment in one of its units to relinquish authority for decision making; it established peer group supervision structures and other in-house innovations to foster a culture of participation and collaboration among its employees. The results convinced the company to expand the program to another unit. Revenues for both units improved dramatically, and the company moved toward a more widespread adoption of this system.

A 2009 study reported in the Harvard Business Review by A. D. Amar, Carsten Hentrich, and Vlatka Hlupic suggested that this example and others provide evidence that a manager's more reliable path to success is not in issuing edicts and monitoring how those edicts are carried out, but in creating a culture in which all employees feel they have a stake in the company's performance, an idea, we recall, that is so important to the millennials who are about to make up the bulk of the workforce. The study called the more open approach "mutualism," the practice of delegating both responsibility and authority to smaller units in the company. For managers used to a more traditional top-down system, such an approach calls for high levels of trust. Pushing trust further and further down the corporate hierarchy and into the hands of more and more people can be incredibly difficult for organizations because it bucks a century's worth of management thinking.[11] But adopting a less hierarchical approach may not be a choice. Leading strategic thinkers from business and government who were participating in a 2010 Aspen Institute Roundtable agreed that businesses face an "unacknowledged crisis" because they, along with government leaders, will have to create an entirely new approach to management and a vision for succeeding in a networked and decentralized world.

Getting this balance right—breaking down hierarchies and giving more control to individuals while maintaining management's ability to boldly lead—represents one of the biggest challenges, but also one of the greatest opportunities, of the Naked Economy.

Philip Rosedale is the first to say it's a tough sell to convince hidebound companies that giving up control is a good move for employee happiness, company productivity, and the bottom line. Many managers have their professional identities deeply wrapped up in the status quo of top-down decision making. "It's really tough sledding getting that stuff sold into organizations," he said. But Philip is a big believer in the anthropological observational approach to figuring out how people behave in organizations. Pointing to the example of Coffee & Power and what he's learned by watching individuals collaborate for their individual and mutual benefit, as well as his experience with needing to boldly and sometimes dictatorially lead his company, Philip sees plenty of potential benefit in getting this balance right. And he's fascinated by the fact that, in his estimation, Silicon Valley has more than its fair share of examples of this balance.

> When we look at the future of work, why is it that so much of the world's software is being built right here in Silicon Valley? And that discrepancy is widening rather than narrowing. What is it that's going on here? We got really interested in these questions. The answer we came up with is that the density of people working on software projects together is ten times higher here than anywhere else in the world. Plus, there is something about this place that creates a culture of sharing. People share here. And when you have those two factors, the density of people doing the same thing, and the fact that people are willing to share with you, you have a much greater likelihood here to find people who will fund you, hire you, work for you, or start something with you.

In other words, people still need people—lots and lots of people, it turns out—in physical proximity to one another for innovation to occur. So now Philip is leaving the virtual world of Second Life behind to take the Love Machine concept outside Linden Lab and into the very human arena of coworking spaces, and, he hopes, into the world beyond. The same ideas of eliminating hierarchies and putting people first, he reckons, can apply to freelancers and independent workers. And giving these otherwise unconnected people a mechanism to collaborate, interact, and share love is the key to unlocking their individual and collective capacity for productivity and innovation. "If someone does something for you, collaborates with you, or provides value to you, you can send them love via the Love Machine. And you can tie that action to a certain skill, which can be linked, say, to their LinkedIn profile, so the rest of the world won't have to guess at what their skills might be or how they've used those skills to create value in the world," he said.[12] The far-reaching conclusion to this line of linking is pretty bold. Imagine a single, global, conscious business organization completely devoid of traditional hierarchies that relies on the horizontal interactions and mutual trust of our most important renewable natural resource: people.

Creating new people-centric work structures can in turn create new corporate values and value. But managers and executives have to learn to trust that newly empowered employees will do the right thing and act for the good of the company even at the expense of the individual.

A lesson in such idealism comes from New Belgium. The Brewery is involved in wind power, smart-grid technology, carbon-capture technology, water conservation, recycling building materials, and other practices. The chairs in the Brewery's tasting room are made of old bicycle rims, to name one recycling innovation at the Fort Collins plant.

In 1998, however, when the company was struggling to establish its various environmentally friendly policies, the employees were called on to make a significant sacrifice.

The employees were asked to vote on whether the company should convert to wind power for its electrical needs. Jeff Lebesch, New Belgium's cofounder, laid out all the benefits to the company for such a plan in terms of reduced carbon emissions, energy savings, and the green brand. The catch was a big one—the plan had to be financed from the employees' bonus pool, meaning no one was getting bonuses for several years.

Bryan Simpson had only recently started at New Belgium at the time. In fact, he had been thinking about returning to his career in broadcast journalism. "I thought it would be a super contentious meeting. But we took the vote, and it was a unanimous thumbs-up vote. And that sealed the deal for me right there at that moment. I thought, you know, these people are here for the right reasons. So I committed at that point in my life to stay here and enjoy what's going on here."

Indeed, as we stand on the verge of the Naked Economy, we have no choice but to cheer on the experiment in self-government that the workers at New Belgium are engaged in, and the company's insistence on keeping people at the center of business. By its sustainable business practices, its commitment to community, and its reliance on its workforce for the wisdom in its decision making, New Belgium is creating a model the business world can point to for what can be.

The inputs to business processes will continue to shift over time. But to one degree or another the implementation of those processes will always be left up to people. In fact for many businesses the only inputs are the ideas, creativity, innovation, and passions of people. As we saw with Philip's Love Machine, technology can be an enabler of the process. But technology evolves much faster than people do. And when we strip away the technology, we're left with just . . . us. Resurrecting the lost art and science of taking care of ourselves and each other may be the most prized, important, and necessary skill as we move forward in the Naked Economy.

CHAPTER 8

PLACE

Welcome to Work, Come Back When You Can't Stay So Long

A revolution can be neither made nor stopped. The only thing that can be done is for one of several of its children to give it a direction by dint of victories.

—Napoleon

A MAN WITHOUT A DESK

Kevin Kuske doesn't have a desk at work. Rather than spend his workday sitting in a single dedicated space, he usually works at various spots around the office that provide the same experience as a desk. You might find Kevin and his colleagues sitting on a pair of facing couches, scribbling on a rolling white board as they brainstorm new ideas. When Kevin needs to work more formally, he has a choice of conference rooms, all equipped with the latest videoconferencing technology. And his favorite place to work is at a big, bar-height table near the office kitchen (fact: sooner or later every party ends up in the kitchen) over snacks and coffee, sometimes alone and focused, more often in groups of two or three with colleagues coming and going as the work and the conversation flows.

Kevin's work environment may sound like the office of a swanky, high-priced marketing firm or a well-funded technology start-up. But it's not. Where does this man-without-a-desk work? The answer is surprising: Kevin Kuske is the general manager of an office furniture company.

Kevin leads Turnstone, a brand of Steelcase, the largest office furniture company in the world. In his LinkedIn profile Kevin calls himself the "Chief Trouble Maker," which gives you an idea of the disruptive ethos that pervades Turnstone. As the nature of work rapidly evolved away from focused individual work to collaborative group work, Kevin and his team saw that most office furniture companies were still cranking out the same old products: big desks, lots of shelves and filing cabinets, fancy chairs with a dozen points of adjustment, and vast seas of office cubicles. The design of products like these assumes that people work all day, every day, in one fixed location. In a manufacturing economy dominated by assembly lines, individuals working in fixed locations was the norm. But since the late twentieth century, the nature of work has evolved rapidly as the Naked Economy begins to take hold. However, the "infrastructure of work"—from the cubicle we sit in to the corporate campus we commute to—hasn't changed much at all. Until now.

GOODBYE DILBERT: THE DEATH OF THE CUBICLE FARM

The workplace revolution is moving fast. And it's picking up steam at an exponential pace. From coffee shops crowded with digital nomads busily tapping away on their laptops to corporate campuses free of assigned workspaces to the sidelines of your kid's soccer game to one of the hundreds of new coworking spaces popping up nearly every day, work is now everywhere.

The forces behind these changes are many: the rapid adoption of mobile technology, ubiquitous Internet access, and a general sense of malaise powered by the vague yet nagging notion that we're just not meant to work all day sitting in a cubicle. Couple technology with employees who are demanding more flexible schedules so they have time for more than just work in their lives. Finally, add the realization that commuting 45 minutes in a car by yourself along traffic-choked highways to sit by yourself in a cubicle for nine hours, then reversing the process to get home, sounds like the kind of thing that happens in a bad Kafka novel.

Motivated by these forces, we're in the midst of a once-in-a-century shift in where we work. Indeed we can work everywhere. But not everywhere works. The man who identified that conundrum is Mark Greiner, the chief experience officer at Steelcase and a colleague of Kevin Kuske's. Mark's job at Steelcase is to push the envelope for the company, focusing on the "now, near, and far" in an effort to keep Steelcase's products on the cutting edge. Mark has an amazingly diverse team of people working for him, including engineers, scientists, anthropologists, sociologists, and designers. Mark and his team also tap into some big brains at the world's leading research universities, including MIT and Georgia Tech. And they collaborate with some of the biggest companies in the world, including IBM, Cisco, and Microsoft. With this intellectual firepower behind him, Mark has spent the past couple of decades thinking deeply about how, where, and why we work.

In the mid-2000s Mark's team began to see two major shifts in work. The first was a shift toward mobility. Companies began to invest heavily in equipping their employees with the latest technology: laptop computers, mobile phones, and the batteries that power them (Mark is quick to remind us of the critical importance of long-lasting, rechargeable batteries, the unsung heroes of the mobile revolution). Companies were not motivated to make these huge capital investments because they were trying to create a mobile workforce. Instead they were merely trying to make cyclical upgrades to their technology; laptops and PDAs—and later, cell phones—were simply what the manufacturers had on offer. The mobility that came with that technology, Mark said with a smile, was a completely unforeseen accident.[1]

With their newfangled toys, employees began to do something that management was completely unprepared for: work everywhere except where they were supposed to work. Caught slightly flat-footed, companies tried to adopt a range of policies that governed mobile work. But the workhorse had already left the barn. And most companies, in Mark's estimation, have been trying to catch up ever since.

The second big trend that Mark and his team observed was a shift from individual work to group work. For the last half-century much of the work in the information economy has been individual, linear, and procedural. Companies set up their offices to accommodate this kind of work. The most iconic example, of course, is the cubicle farm. As soul deadening as many of us now regard the cubicle farm, it was an efficient work space solution for the individual, linear, procedural work that most companies were doing. Cube farms were information factories where workers, in assembly-line fashion reminiscent of our industrial roots, moved information from in-basket to in-basket. In the last half of the twentieth century, companies made enormous capital investments in building, furnishing, provisioning, and managing these information factories. And when companies make those kinds of investments, they expect to get long useful lives out of them. So the cube farm endures. But not for long.

Why? Since the early part of the new century much of that individual, linear, procedural work has been outsourced, sent offshore, and automated. The work that remains is largely creative and conceptual, and the problems that companies are now asking their employees to solve are big, complex, and far reaching. The solutions can't be found on a spreadsheet or through a fancy regression analysis. Instead these problems require, in Mark Greiner's words, the "perspectives of many." The solutions to these problems will emerge when lots of people from different disciplines and with varied skills come together to work. In other words, we're replacing the individual, linear, procedural information economy with the group, creative, conceptual innovation economy.

Take these two trends together—the rise of mobility in the workforce and the shift from individual linear work to collaborative group work—and we can draw only one conclusion: what we've come to know as the traditional workplace is irrelevant and outdated. Scott Adams, the genius behind *Dilbert*, and sitcom writers everywhere are going to have to find some new material.

THE RISE OF THE WORKPLACE ECOSYSTEM

So you've got a smart phone and a laptop. Maybe you've got a slick tablet computer, too. Your cell phone provider has ensured that you get a strong four-bar signal pretty much everywhere. And when you flip open that laptop, about a dozen wi-fi networks are at your disposal. You've got a meeting with a couple of your colleagues and a new client to dive into the big project that you're working on. Where do you work?

The answer (and it's not as glib as it sounds): It depends. It depends on what kind of technology you need access to, remembering that something as simple as a white board still counts as technology. It depends on whether you and your team need privacy. It depends on what kind of vibe you and your team need: something that resembles a library reading room or more like a bustling street corner? It also depends on whether it's a nice day and the idea of sitting cooped up in the office sounds like a completely wasted opportunity to go for a run or take your kids to the park; after all, why can't I respond to e-mail, review work for a client, or download that quarterly report at home after the kids have gone to bed? Since the traditional workplace is irrelevant and outdated, we really need to ask a different question. Rather than "Where should we work?" a key question of the Naked Economy becomes, "Given what we need to accomplish right now, what kind of setting do we need so that we can work at our creative, innovative, and productive best?"

The answer also depends on whether you actually have a job. In this case we're not talking about the ranks of the unemployed, which still hovered at about 9 percent of the workforce as of this writing. Instead we're talking about the growing number of freelancers, independent consultants, and other brains-for-hire, many of whom we've already met. The ranks of these "contingent workers" are growing incredibly fast. In 2010 the software company Intuit conducted a study called the "Intuit 2020 Report: Twenty Trends That Will Shape the Next Decade." In the report Intuit asks us to imagine a world where contingent work is as common as traditional employment. That world is nearly here: by 2020 more than 40 percent of the US workforce will be contingent workers.[2] These workers—what we call the "disaggregated workforce"—don't have regular jobs so they don't need a fixed, company-provided workplace. Their answer to the question of where to work depends on who's hired their brains today.

For most of the last 100 years we didn't have to answer this question of where to work. We got jobs, we showed up at the office every day, and we did our thing. But Mark Gilbreath, the CEO of a start-up called LiquidSpace, is building a company based on the idea that work is no longer a single place. Instead work is a real-time decision that we make when we answer all those "it depends" questions. And, as the answers to those questions change in an hour/day/week, so too will our choices of where to work. Given this new fluid characteristic of the workplace, LiquidSpace is a particularly appropriate name for Mark's company.

At its center LiquidSpace is a mobile application accessed with a smart phone that allows users to "choose a better place to work today." Understanding that work is now a real-time decision, Mark's team built the application to be, first, location aware, meaning your smart phone knows where you are and feeds that information into the app, and, second, adjustable according to the sort of work environment you need. Users can control dials based on how many people they need to work with, ranging from 1 to 50; the kind of infrastructure they need, everything from office business centers to libraries to public parks to coffee shops to hotel lobbies to unused offices within a corporate campus to coworking spaces; and the kind of vibe they're looking for, with clever labels like "JetSetter," "Impress," "Cone of Silence," and "Room with a View." Taking these three variables into account—location, infrastructure, and vibe— LiquidSpace generates a list of nearby work spaces, most of which look absolutely nothing like the traditional office.

The real genius of LiquidSpace is the idea that for many of us the workplace has become an ecosystem of places that we access on a real-time, on-demand basis. This idea is a natural extension of the trends that Steelcase's Mark Greiner uncovered: the rise in mobility and the shift from individual linear work to collaborative group work. Mobility and the need for collaboration, coupled with the rise of the disaggregated workforce, have led many of us to seek out the workplace conditions that will allow us to be at our innovative, creative, and productive best right now. As the nature of the actual work that we need to accomplish changes, day to day and sometimes even minute to minute, we're slowly evolving into a seminomadic workforce, constantly ranging from corporate office to coffee shop to coworking space, seeking the perfect combination of location, infrastructure, and vibe. No wonder Kevin Kuske doesn't need a desk.

Unfortunately, many of our current choices don't provide the perfect, or even an acceptable combination of location, infrastructure, and vibe so that we can be at our creative, innovative, and productive best. For the disaggregated workforce the most obvious choice of workplace is the home. At first blush working at home seems like the perfect solution. The commute is short, the dress code is liberal, and that creepy guy from the accounting department is nowhere to be found. But if we look at the home through the lens of our three workplace variables, working from home quickly breaks down as a viable solution. Location? Again, you can't beat the commute from your bedroom to your kitchen. You get to keep your carbon footprint low, and you regain the 30 to 90 minutes that most of us spend commuting. Infrastructure? Your laptop and your home Internet connection are great for most tasks. But most of us are a little uncomfortable inviting a team of work colleagues into our kitchen. Also, your home probably lacks, say, the white boards and projectors you might need for effective collaborative work. Vibe? This is where the allure of working from home really loses its luster. As we surveyed the work-from-home crowd, the biggest reason they quickly tired of the home office was loneliness. Sitting alone in your living room (your cat doesn't count) in your loungewear with *The Ellen DeGeneres Show* blaring in the background might not be the best backdrop for being at your creative, innovative, and productive best. However, we shouldn't completely abandon the home as a workplace. Instead we should simply see working at home as part of our larger workplace ecosystem.

When working from home doesn't work, the next place most of us venture in search of the perfect combination of location, infrastructure, and vibe is the coffee shop. Coffee shops are everywhere. In many places they're more than everywhere. In our hometown of Santa Cruz, California (population 57,000), no fewer than five coffee shops occupy a one-block stretch of Pacific Avenue, the main drag through downtown. The ubiquity of coffee shops is a big reason why they've become such an iconic part of our workplace ecosystem; from a location perspective coffee shops fit our workplace needs well. They fall short, however, in terms of infrastructure. After all, they're coffee shops, presumably designed for the preparation, sale, and enjoyment of, um, coffee. In most coffee shops the furniture isn't designed for long periods of sitting, the tables aren't designed as ideal work surfaces, and the wi-fi often isn't secure or reliable. Holding a meeting or taking a phone call while the baristas loudly foam milk in your ears or the college kids at the next table yak away . . . well, that's hardly the professional atmosphere most of us need.

Yet we still flock to coffee shops, laptops and tablet computers tucked under our arms, hoping to get some work done. Why? The biggest reason coffee shops are such popular workspaces is that they begin to fulfill our need for a conducive workplace vibe. In our surveys we found that people used words like *buzz*, *hum*, and *energy* when describing why they worked at coffee shops. Further, they said that the lack of this energy was the biggest reason why working from home wasn't optimal. If the goal is to find a workplace where we can be at our creative, innovative, and productive best, the buzz and energy of a coffee shop help to fuel all that creativity and innovation. The caffeine probably doesn't hurt our productivity, either.

However, coffee shop owners are beginning to revolt. Tired of the digital squatters who camp out for hours on end nursing a single latte, some coffee shop owners have taken draconian measures to reclaim their space. Some turn their wi-fi off on the weekends, while some have turned it off altogether. Another clever strategy is covering up the power outlets. The message: Feel free to sit here and work as long as you'd like, but when your laptop battery dies, go somewhere else. The owner of Four Barrel Coffee in San Francisco removed all the real outlets from his coffee shop and painted fake power outlets on the walls, then got a kick out of watching the confused looks as the owners of power-hungry laptops jabbed their plugs at the drywall.

Nonetheless, coffee shops will probably continue to be part of our workplace ecosystem for some time. Their ubiquity and convenience, coupled with our insatiable collective need for caffeine, make them an easy place to get a few hours' work done. Hanging out in a coffee shop is an old tradition: the very first European coffee shops—they began cropping up around the Austrian Empire in the early nineteenth century— were places where writers, thinkers, merchants, poets, philosophers, and madmen often gathered. When this motley mixture of characters got together and rubbed shoulders, sparks often flew. Some say the revolutions of 1848—the first and only widespread political upheaval to affect nearly all of Europe—started in the coffee shops of Vienna. Hey, if a coffee shop is a good place to launch a widespread political revolution, then it's only fitting that it's also a good place to launch a revolution in where, how, and why we work.

LOCATION + INFRASTRUCTURE + VIBE = COWORKING

So where is this workplace revolution leading us? As a workforce we're more mobile than ever. We're also more disaggregated than ever as many of us transition, either by choice or because of a still-crappy economy, from full-time employment to being freelancers and independent consultants. The kind of work we need to do requires collaborating with others. But none of the workplace choices that we've looked at so far—the outdated corporate office, our homes, and the corner coffee shop—provide the location, infrastructure, and vibe we need to be at our creative, innovative, and productive best. The inadequacy of the modern workplace stands as perhaps the most iconic reminder of the challenges we face in the Naked Economy.

And whenever an industry sector is ripe for change, you can always count on scrappy entrepreneurial types to come up with an industry-disrupting solution. The most interesting and disruptive workplace solution we've seen is the emergence of coworking. Obviously, while our opinions about coworking are a little biased, the meteoric rise of this new way to work, the attention it's gotten in the popular press, and the rush to emulate the coworking model in other industry sectors makes us more than comfortable with singing the praises of this new and powerful workplace trend.

So what is coworking? Ask a dozen coworking space operators and you're likely to get a dozen different answers (this ambiguity is indicative of the promise of coworking; it's still an emerging idea that's being developed in real time and can be tailored to solve different workplace challenges). But most will agree on a definition that looks something like this: Coworking is a way of working in which freelancers, independent professionals, telecommuters, start-ups, and others with workplace flexibility share a single work environment, placing emphasis on the values of collaboration, openness, community, accessibility, and sustainability.

While the idea of shared collaborative workspaces is centuries old, we date the modern iteration of coworking from 2005 in San Francisco. There, a freelance technology worker named Brad Neuberg opened the Hat Factory, a live-work space that was also open to independent workers who were looking for a better combination of location, infrastructure, and vibe. The idea wasn't simply to share workspace. Instead coworking grew out of a need for independent workers to connect, collaborate, exchange ideas, share expertise, and, they hoped, create the conditions to work at their creative, productive, and innovative best. In other words, what Brad and his fellow co-workers were really hungry for was this important but elusive idea of community.

Now is a good time to take a short anthropological detour and think about the rise, fall, and rise of human communities. When we swung down from the trees, we quickly discovered that if we worked together as part of a strong, collaborative community, we had an easier time hunting mammoths, building villages, and raising our kids. And this idea of creating and sustaining communities worked well for the better part of 100,000 years. But by the middle of the twentieth century, our communities—at least in the United States and other industrialized countries—had begun to fray. Robert Putnam, a professor at Harvard's Kennedy School of Government, identified this phenomenon in his groundbreaking 2000 book *Bowling Alone: The Collapse and Revival of the American Community.*[3]

The rise of social networking has reconnected us in ways never before imaginable. For good or ill, we can now follow the daily dramas of every one of our kindergarten classmates. But we can also mobilize and organize disparate groups of people, share memories with distant loved ones, and generally keep in touch with a wide range of personal and professional connections. As powerful as social networking tools like Facebook, Twitter, and LinkedIn are, they are flawed because they cannot be substitutes for the real, live, genuine, physical community that we've evolved to rely on, but is so sorely lacking in our modern society. The cover story for the May 2012 edition of the *Atlantic* magazine—"Is Facebook Making Us Lonely?"—spoke to this problem.[4]

While Steelcase's Mark Greiner is correct in his assertion that work is moving from individual linear tasks to group collaborative tasks, something much more fundamental is also going on in our society: people are hungry—desperate, even—for real, live, genuine, physical community. Satisfying this hunger is perhaps the greatest power of the coworking industry. And a return to working with these kinds of communities is perhaps the most powerful tool we have in unlocking the promise of the Naked Economy.

Let's look at coworking through the three lenses of location, infrastructure, and vibe. Acknowledging the value of accessibility, most coworking spaces are located in areas of high population density, often within the downtown urban core of cities with a high degree of walkability. Many are located close to public transportation and/or help their members with alternative transportation solutions, like providing ample bike parking; NextSpace provides its members with discounted memberships to Zipcar, the car-sharing service that began the revolution in collaborative consumption. In many ways coworking is the antidote to long commutes to the corporate campus in single-occupant, carbon-belching cars.

The infrastructure within a coworking space varies. The individual spaces range in size from a few hundred square feet to tens of thousands of square feet. The furnishings and decor can range from high end to Ikea chic. Most coworking spaces have some combination of private offices, shared conference rooms, kitchen facilities, and open, collaborative spaces filled with desks and couches. In a coworking space the only thing more important than fast, reliable, commercial-grade broadband Internet bandwidth is coffee, the lifeblood of the Naked Economy (one of our favorite company aphorisms: a NextSpace member is the universe's way of turning caffeine into awesome).

A key part of coworking is the flexibility of the workplace infrastructure. Depending on the task at hand, our workplace infrastructure requirements can quickly vary. One moment we need privacy to take that all-important phone call or to do some quiet focused work. The next moment we need openness, collaboration, and access to a variety of different people to get feedback on a new idea. And the next moment we need to meet with a small team to move a project forward. The best coworking spaces provide a range of infrastructure to accommodate these constantly varying workstyles: individual desks, big tables for group work, couches and other comfy furniture for daydreaming and for the thinking of big thoughts, phone booths for private calls, conference rooms of various shapes and sizes, and lots and lots and lots of white boards.

Another key aspect of the flexibility of coworking has to do with how members—particularly the freelancers, entrepreneurs, independent consultants, and other participants in the disaggregated workforce—access a coworking space. For a long time the only way for these disaggregated workers to get access to an office was to rent one. However, renting an office is a risky proposition. Most landlords require long-term lease commitments and often require tenants to put up their personal assets—like their houses or their retirement savings—as collateral in case they can't make the rent payments. For freelancers and entrepreneurs, who often work from project to project or gig to gig, taking on this kind of risk is a bad business decision (and another reason why so many work from home or in coffee shops). But most coworking spaces sell month-to-month memberships, and many provide options for day-to-day or hour-to-hour access to the space. This on-demand access to the space is a major driver of the success of coworking.

The strongest attraction of coworking comes in the form of our third workplace attribute: vibe. For many of us the vibe of working at the corporate campus can be pretty stale. The vibe of working from home is one of loneliness and isolation. And the vibe of working at a coffee shop is one of noise and unprofessionalism. At NextSpace, as at many coworking spaces, we aim for a vibe that is welcoming, comfortable, and professional. And, above all, we aim for a vibe that simultaneously screams for and subtly suggests collaboration and community. Why? As an increasingly disaggregated workforce, we work at our creative, innovative, and productive best when we reaggregate into a community, feed off each other's energy, share ideas, refer business to each other, and combine talents to create new products, services, and solutions.

In 2012 *Deskmag*, an online magazine dedicated to coworking, conducted its second annual coworking survey. With 1,500 people from 52 countries participating, *Deskmag*'s survey is the most comprehensive look at the emerging coworking industry. Two statistics from the survey stand out. First is the enormous growth in coworking in a short amount of time. In 2006 the number of coworking spaces worldwide was 30; in 2011 it was 1,130 (projections for 2012 are 2,150). Second is the importance that coworkers put on collaboration and community. Eighty-four percent of coworkers said they found interaction with other people an important aspect of their work; 82 percent said that random discoveries and opportunities—what others have called "accelerated serendipity"—is an important part of the coworking experience.[5] The reaggregation of the workforce into a strong collaborative community stands as one of coworking's greatest benefits.

THE NEXTSPACE EFFECT

At NextSpace we have a special name for the results of this community-based reaggregation: the NextSpace Effect. The NextSpace Effect comes in many varieties and runs along a spectrum. At one end of the spectrum is the purely social aspect of being a member of NextSpace's coworking community. Meeting other people in a professional, collaborative environment beats the isolation of working from home or the chaos of working at a coffee shop. At the other end of the spectrum are the tangible business results that come from interacting with people who have complementary skill sets.

In terms of tangible business results, our favorite example of the NextSpace Effect is the story of Rally Up. Sol Lipman, a 30-something entrepreneur and a veteran of the Silicon Valley start-up scene, joined NextSpace in early 2009. While working at NextSpace, he met several other members who had interests and skills that were similar to but—and this is important—not exactly the same as his. In the spirit of the Smart Generalist-Super Specialist dichotomy that is a hallmark of the Naked Economy, Sol gathered together this seemingly disparate group of independent workers: a graphic designer, a project manager, a few programmers, and a couple of mobile application developers. They set to work creating Rally Up, a social network that allows users to send status updates via their smart phones to a small group of "real friends." Rally Up quickly garnered attention in the national press, and, in typical Silicon Valley fashion, the tech giant AOL acquired Rally Up for a nice seven-figure payday.

Rally Up is a headline-grabbing version of the NextSpace Effect. But stories like this, in large and small ways, happen in coworking spaces every day across the world. Maybe a web developer meets a graphic designer; together they make a client's website look sleek and professional. Maybe a freelance writer meets an independent attorney; together they ensure that the freelancer's contracts provide adequate legal protections, with the freelancer paying a fraction of the fees a big law firm might charge (or perhaps they make a trade: legal consultation in exchange for spiffy new written copy on the lawyer's website). Maybe a business strategy consultant meets a marketing pro; together they tackle a big project for an important customer. This "better together" mentality and self-organization into strong, collaborative communities are the ultimate manifestation of location, infrastructure, and vibe so critical to the success of the new workplace.

"WELCOME TO WORK! NOW GET OUT!"

We've seen that the typical corporate workplace—that ubiquitous cubicle farm that we all love to hate—no longer fits the trend toward collaborative group work. In search of other options many of us have retreated to our homes or flocked to local coffee shops. When those options proved unsatisfactory, coworking emerged as a viable solution, although it is still in its infancy. So the revolution of the workplace is underway. What will sustain it?

To answer that question we need to return briefly to the cubicle farm. Of course we may be the only ones returning. And when we get there, here's who we're likely to bump into: no one. Another fact from Mark Greiner's research is the staggering underuse of the typical corporate campus. During two-thirds of the average workday, the typical office space is empty.

By now we shouldn't be terribly surprised by that statistic. Why would people show up to work at place that doesn't fit their needs? Employees have already begun voting with their feet, finding better work space solutions on their own. Now corporate real estate professionals and facilities managers look around their empty buildings and wonder where everyone has gone; they have begun to dive into this issue of underused space, trying to understand, and maybe get on board with, the revolution of the workplace.

One such enlightened person is Ed Nolan. Ed worked for the tech giant Hewlett Packard for almost 30 years, the last 13 as the head of HP's workplace strategy. Ed spent an entire career thinking about how a big company like HP can provide a variety of work spaces to its employees. Now, perhaps tellingly, Ed works for Mark Gilbreath's team at LiquidSpace, where Ed tries to convince corporate real estate managers to think differently about how they provide the location, infrastructure, and vibe that their employees need to be at their creative, innovative, and productive best.

Ed divides the recent history of the corporate real estate profession into two categories: Portfolio 1.0 and Portfolio 2.0. As Ed describes it, "Portfolio 1.0 was a supply-driven model for providing work space, encompassing the buildings and work spaces owned or leased by a company." This portfolio of real estate and work space assets, including those pesky cube farms, is what we think of as the traditional workplace. The job of a company's real estate portfolio manager and facilities director was to "doggedly pursue the optimization of utilizing these assets, measuring success by the actual usage of their company-controlled assets." If usage is the metric for success, the persistent underuse of the typical corporate campus is perhaps the final nail in the coffin of the traditional office work space.

Portfolio 2.0 is a demand-driven work space model. Rather than supply its employees with a corporate campus and hope they use it, corporate real estate professionals in Portfolio 2.0 try to provide employees with the options and the flexibility they need to find the perfect combination of location, infrastructure, and vibe. Those options may exist at the corporate campus, and many companies (we'll meet one in a moment) are quickly moving to redesign their real estate assets to be more suitable for group and collaborative work. Or those companies may give their people the options we've already explored: working from home, the coffee shop, a coworking space, hotel lobby, or even a blanket spread out on a beach. As Ed put it, "In the Portfolio 2.0 model, we move away from optimizing physical assets and towards optimizing human productivity."[6]

That shift has profound implications for sustaining the workplace revolution. The first is a reconsideration of what to do with existing corporate real estate assets and the dreaded cube farms that many still contain. Companies make enormous long-term investments in these assets. They sign long-term leases or buy the buildings outright, then spend six or seven figures furnishing and outfitting them. If these assets are underused for two-thirds of the typical workday, the typical corporate campus amounts to a pile of wasted money that's not easily recoverable. Forward-thinking companies are coming up with innovative ways to redeploy these assets. One such company is Plantronics, a consumer electronics company with a long history of manufacturing headsets; now it makes Blue Tooth headsets for use with smart phones (fun fact: the late, great Neil Armstrong wore a Plantronics headset while walking on the moon). Plantronics recently completed a total redesign of its corporate work spaces, getting rid of the cubicles, increasing the number of conference rooms, adding lots of open "touchdown" space and first-come-first-served desk space, and installing flat screen monitors throughout its buildings. This last addition makes it easier to videoconference with teammates who are working outside the corporate campus.

And, as it turns out, lots of Plantronics employees will be working outside the corporate campus. Why? Because the campus is designed to accommodate a maximum of 60 percent of Plantronics' employees at any given time. Indeed management anticipates that a different 60 percent will show up for work on any given day, while the other 40 percent opt to work somewhere else. Plantronics is not alone in having this insight. Major companies are planning, budgeting, and designing their offices on this metric.

Where is that someplace else? It's the ecosystem of real-time, on-demand work spaces that we've already examined. Certainly, many Plantronics employees are working at home, getting some work done at a customer's or client's site, or checking e-mails at a local coffee shop. And, for a significant chunk of the Plantronics workforce, one of our NextSpace co-working spaces in downtown San Jose, California, is an important part of the workplace ecosystem. Perhaps more than any other company, Plantronics is on the cutting edge of setting its employees free, giving them a variety of work space options to choose from.

These work space strategy decisions have some tangible by-products. In addition to creating a workplace where his employees are more innovative and happy, by executing this strategy Plantronics's CEO, Ken Kannappan, estimates that his company will save more than $4 million annually on reduced real estate overhead expenses. Those savings drop straight to the company's bottom line. That's great for Plantronics, but it's just a drop in the bucket compared to the aggregate potential savings that companies could realize by adopting Portfolio 2.0 work space strategies. For example, a study by the architecture firm Gensler found that, in some high-priced real estate markets, a typical corner office can cost a company more than $75,000 per year.[7] And that's just for the real estate, not the furniture, IT infrastructure, and other trappings of a modern office. Reducing or even eliminating this pricey overhead and giving employees a choice of where to work not only makes the employees happier and more productive, it can save the company a bundle of money.

This company-sanctioned choice of work space leads to the second major implication of the shift from the asset-based real estate management of Portfolio 1.0 to the productivity-based management of Portfolio 2.0. When companies give their employees the freedom to make real-time work space decisions, they have effectively consumerized the work space. Instead of procuring work space at the wholesale level by leasing or purchasing big corporate campuses, companies like Plantronics are letting their employees procure work space at the retail level through the real-time decisions these employees make to find that perfect mix of location, infrastructure, and vibe.

This consumerization of the work space is not unlike the recent trend in the consumerization of information technology. Instead of buying huge numbers of, say, computers and complex telephone systems for their employees' use, companies have begun letting their employees purchase whatever laptop or smart phone they're most comfortable with, often providing them an allowance to do so. The same is true of enterprise software. Why invest millions of dollars in huge installations of enterprise software when employees can pick the software—often web-based software than can be accessed free of charge—that allows them to be the most productive?

Smart companies are asking themselves a similar question about work space. Why invest millions of dollars in procuring work space that employees don't use when those employees— viewing the world through the perspective of the work space ecosystem that we've developed—can make better, smarter, and less expensive work space decisions on their own? The acceleration of this trend toward consumerization will sustain the workplace revolution as the Naked Economy continues to pick up steam.

What might the future of the consumerized work space look like? Imagine showing up for your first day of work at a new company. Instead of issuing you your computer, activating your new smart phone, and showing you to your new desk, the company simply hands you a stack of money. And with that money you're meant to buy the technology you need to get your job done as well as purchase access to the range of work spaces you'll likely need to be at your creative, innovative, and productive best. With the work space portion of that allowance, you may join a coworking space like NextSpace. You may purchase a fancy new chair for your home office. Or you may buy just enough lattes to prevent the local coffee shop owner from kicking you to the curb as you merrily tap away on your laptop. Or, most likely, you'll do all three. And then some.

But we can make an even further imaginative leap as we think about the consumerization of the work space. Suppose you actually do want to work at the corporate campus for a day or two. Maybe there's a particular piece of technology, like a high-end videoconferencing system, that you need to use. Or maybe you need to impress an important client, and the corporate campus has several chic conference rooms designed to do just that. Or maybe you and your team need to hole up for a few weeks in a dedicated project area to do some deep thinking about a critical problem. If you need to use these kinds of facilities at the corporate campus, the company may very well charge you for the privilege. That's right: you receive a work space allowance from your company, then turn around and give part of that allowance back in order to work at the company's facilities.

Sound strange? This idea is strange only when we view the workplace through the old asset-based model. But if we view the workplace through the consumerized, productivity-based model that encourages employees to make their own work space decisions, the corporate campus must compete against all the other choices contained within the workplace ecosystem. The corporate campus will have to compete with the home office, coffee shop, coworking space, and perhaps dozens of other work space alternatives to provide the perfect combination of location, infrastructure, and community that people need to be at their creative, innovative, and productive best.

With all this in mind, a new term-of-art is beginning to take hold to describe the shift away from the asset-based work space model to the consumerized productivity model of the workspace: work space as a service (WaaS). Much like the shift from product-based to service-based software, WaaS is on demand and flexible. Jay Baughman is the president of the Global Workspace Association, an international trade association whose mission is to advance work space as a service. Jay thinks about WaaS this way: "The workplace is no longer a decision to be made within the corporate real estate department. Instead it's a business strategy decision to be made in the company boardroom."[8] The movement toward the flexible WaaS strategy has widespread effects that pervade all aspects of the business: employee recruitment and retention, productivity, carbon footprint, management and human resources, and ultimately the bottom line. Getting these decisions right, consumerizing the work space, and allowing workers to decide for themselves how they can be the most happy and productive are absolutely essential as we move forward in the Naked Economy.

THE PAPER TABLE

The consumerization of the workplace and the beginning of the workplace revolution bring us back to Kevin Kuske, our hero without a desk. We have caught up in person with Kevin, along with his chief of sales at Turnstone, Jeff Schutte. We're gathered, along with several hundred other people in the work space-as-a-service industry, in Baltimore, at the annual conference of the Global Workspace Association. Always eager to kick around some new ideas, particularly about something as revolutionary as the future of the workplace, three of us are seated around an especially unrevolutionary object: a pad of paper.

Of course this is no ordinary pad of paper. It's big and round, about 24 inches in diameter, so there's plenty of space for sketching and scribbling. It's set into the top of a low table, about 25 inches high, which allows us to quickly gather around it seated on three comfy ottomans. The table also rotates, allowing us to spin the pad so we can add to and build on the ideas that we're brainstorming together. Feeding off each other's creative energy—we communicate by phone and e-mail fairly frequently, but this is the first time we've been together in person for almost a year—we begin to incorporate the coffee stains and cookie crumbs from our afternoon snack into our doodling. Despite the relaxed atmosphere, or perhaps because of it, we're making great headway on an interesting problem that's been nagging us for months.

What's really revolutionary about the Paper Table is the simplicity of thinking that went into its creation. Kevin, Jeff, and their team apply design thinking when developing new products. They acutely observe human behavior to learn something to help them solve a problem. They're less concerned with the actual products they develop (although their products are really cool) and more concerned with the experience that those products create. In the case of the Paper Table, Jeff and his team were trying to replicate a simple but incredibly powerful experience. In their research they watched people repeatedly gather quickly and informally around all sorts of ad hoc horizontal surfaces for impromptu group work sessions. Grabbing scratch paper, grocery receipts, or the storied cocktail napkin, people found the experience of these informal gatherings an important part of their workplace ecosystem.

More fundamentally, Kevin and Jeff understood that people have been engaging in the kinds of experience that the Paper Table creates . . . forever. "As a species we started solving tough problems hundreds of thousands of years ago by gathering together under a tree and drawing with sticks in the dirt on the savanna. The Paper Table is just another manifestation of an age-old behavior that hasn't really changed much over the millennia."[9]

Think about that: one of Turnstone's most innovative products is designed to mimic a human behavior that developed at
the very beginning of our species. That idea gives us perhaps
our strongest insight into what the workplace ecosystem in the
Naked Economy should look like. We need to strip the workplace bare, get rid of the cubicles and the clunky desks, and replace them with a range of experience-based solutions. "When
you apply design thinking to a problem," Kevin said, "you realize that, at our core, we're really meant to be in harmony with
our surroundings." Indeed the quest to be in harmony with our
surroundings—and to have the individual and collective power
to choose our workplaces in real time—stands as the most elegant and efficient way to find the combination of location,
infrastructure, and vibe that we need to be at our creative, innovative, and productive best.

CHAPTER 9

POLICY

Vote Naked and Other Adventures in Policy

My son is now an entrepreneur. That's what you're called when you don't have a real job.

—Ted Turner

YOU ARE NOT A W-2

Throughout this book, we've introduced a number of rather amazing people who are questioning everything and succeeding on the frontiers of the new workforce. And we'll introduce several more before we conclude. What's more remarkable than these pioneers' achievements is that they've created this success without the help of the System, that amalgamation of federal, state, and local policies that govern how we live and work. As we'll show, the System is heavily geared toward people with "real jobs": those who have full- or part-time work with established companies, receive employer-sponsored benefits (if they're lucky), and get a nice tidy IRS Form W-2 at the end of the year.

As we've already shown, those "real job" people—more power to them—are declining in number both by choice and by necessity. And what people find when they leave the System is a confusing, byzantine, and slightly scary world of health insurance, taxes, pensions, and regulations. In the old economy, companies navigated this landscape on behalf of their employees, often using armies of lawyers, tax accountants, and human resources specialists to make sure employees are insured, regulations are followed, and laws are obeyed. However, when Smart Generalists and Super Specialists courageously step into the Naked Economy, they have to navigate this labyrinth on their own.

As the number of freelancers, independent consultants, and entrepreneurs continues to grow—indeed, as they become the dominant force in the economy—the System will have to adapt and change to meet their needs. The System has adapted to changes in the economy before and will adapt again. The question is how soon we can enact these changes to reflect the Naked Economy. The sooner the better, in our opinion. We make this pronouncement with a straight face, knowing that our country is in the midst of partisan gridlock at every level of government, that systemic change is hard even under the best of circumstances, and that interests vested in maintaining the status quo abound. But we have no choice but to be hopeful. Not only are the free agents you've met in this book relying on it, so is our nation's ability to create a strong, innovative, robust, sustainable economy for the coming century.

WHEN A JOB ISN'T A JOB

A front-page article in the *New York Times* in October 2012 ominously headlined "When Job-Creation Engines Stop at

Just One" exemplifies the failure of the System (and the media) to wrap their mind around the new reality of the Naked Economy.[1] The article was timely because it appeared at the height of the American election season, and both political parties were fighting ferociously about who could create more jobs faster. The stakes were so high in this debate that when the normally uncontroversial Bureau of Labor Statistics released a marginally upbeat jobs report the same day that the article appeared, all hell broke loose. Jack Welch, the former CEO of General Electric, tweeted that the bureau had manipulated the numbers for political ends. Although he was quickly discredited by every major media source, the fact remained that, as a nation, we can't even agree on how to do something as simple as count jobs.

The *Times* article profiled Mike Farmer, a Kansas City entrepreneur who launched a mobile search app called Leap2. Mike is like millions of entrepreneurs around the country: he sees a need in the marketplace, develops a product to meet that need, raises a little bit of investment cash, keeps his costs low, and works hard to give his product a foothold in the virtual marketplace. So what got Mike on the front page of the paper of record? He has no employees.

Rather than hire employees, Mike uses seven independent contractors to do coding, graphic design, market research, marketing, and anything else that needs to get done. The team is based in the Kansas City area, but members mostly interact through Skype and meet once a week for dinner (the only guy from out of the area attends these dinners through Skype with an iPad propped on a chair). Some of the contractors are working full time on Leap2, and most have other projects and jobs. By now we hope this sounds familiar: a project-based team of

Super Specialists coming together on their own terms, led by a Smart Generalist (Mike), to create meaningful work for themselves, develop an innovative product for the global marketplace, and create real value in the economy.

With the unemployment rate stubbornly stuck in the high single digits and with every elected official declaring small business to be more American than Mom and apple pie, Mike's story is one that should be celebrated and emulated. "We need a million more Mike Farmers!" one can imagine a Senate candidate shouting to cheering and adoring crowds.

But instead the article, and the economists interviewed for it, engaged in significant hand-wringing. Emblematic of the concerned tone of the article was Scott Shane, professor of economics at Case Western Reserve University, who observed, "There's this idea that we can somehow rely on entrepreneurship to get us out of the jobs crisis. That's getting harder and harder, considering there are fewer and fewer of them, and they're each employing fewer and fewer people." While his premise is theoretically correct—the Kauffman Foundation found that in 1999, the typical new business created 7.7 new jobs while in 2011 that number had fallen to 4.7—this premise is simply wrong in the real world where most of us, even economists, live.[2]

A job once was an exchange of work for money. And that's exactly what Mike and his contractors are doing. Mike pays these contractors in good old-fashioned American dollars that they can use to buy food, pay rent, and maybe enjoy the occasional night on the town. His company also pays cash to outside vendors for things like office space, computer equipment, web services, and even those weekly dinners. This exchange of work for money—and the secondary exchange that this activity

engenders—is pretty much the definition of a healthy economy. But, for the purposes of counting, the members of Mike's
team don't have "jobs" because they don't fall into a particular
tax status or a particular category on some government survey.
So all the economic activity they create doesn't officially count,
even if it feels like it does to Mike and his team. If we don't even
have policies to effectively count guys like Mike and his team,
in what other ways is our policy infrastructure ill equipped for
the Naked Economy?

No organization has been a bigger champion of freelancers
and free agents than the Freelancers Union, an advocacy group
started by Sara Horowitz (whom we already met briefly in
Chapter 6) in 1999. To say that Sara is a pioneer is an enormous
understatement. Before Freelancers Union no single organization was dedicated to advancing the interests of this enormous
but—at the time—largely invisible section of the workforce.
In just over a decade's time, Freelancers Union has attracted
nearly 200,000 independent workers to its ranks, all of whom,
according to the union's mission statement, are "practical revo-
lutionaries who look for innovative ways to bring together and
support the country's 42 million independent workers."

In 2011 the Freelancers Union published a white paper with
a simple title: "America's Uncounted Independent Workforce."
The white paper cites a 2006 report by the US Government Accountability Office (GAO) that set the number of independent
and contingent workers—contractors, temps, and the self-employed—at 42.6 million, or 30 percent of the American workforce. How many independent and contingent workers are
there today? We don't know. GAO discontinued its "Contingent
Work Supplement" survey in 2005 and hasn't had the budget to
conduct it since. So at a time when the growth of independent

and contingent workers is on the rise, we have no official statistics regarding their numbers, simply because we have failed to count them.

The white paper goes on to make some simple statements that should be blindingly obvious but apparently are completely lost on government policy makers: "Even though they comprise a significant chunk of the economy, it's easy to overlook independent workers' needs since they aren't consistently defined and tracked . . . if the government counted independent workers, [elected officials] could design more effective policies that support what the workforce needs to succeed, thereby supporting our economy."[3]

Imagine what would happen if we reclaimed the notion of jobs from the human resources bureaucracy and returned it to its original purpose: you contribute to society, and you and society benefit. And what better place to start than the single biggest impediment to Mike, his contractors, and virtually everyone trying to work in the Naked Economy: our employer-based health insurance system.

UNHEALTHY HEALTH CARE

Sean McMurray has always loved lighting. "Whenever I walk into a room, I always notice how it's lit. And I'm always amazed at how lighting can completely change a room, change its mood, change its function, and change the people who are in it. It's part art, part science, with a little bit of magic thrown in."

For most of his working life Sean's interest in lighting wasn't much more than a passing thing. From 1996 until 2010 he worked in the electronics industry, rising to become the director of marketing for one of the world's largest distributors of electronics components. It was good work and allowed him the flexibility of working from home and telecommuting several days a week. This flexibility was important to Sean since he has two kids and, like most parents, wants to be an integral part of their lives as they grow up.

A few years ago, Sean found himself heading a team that was tasked with selling LED components to the lighting industry. The popularity of LED lighting was on the rise and business was booming. "LED lights consume 80 percent less energy than regular incandescent bulbs," Sean explained. "They can last up to 20 years in industrial applications and up to 50 years in residential applications. Plus, they don't contain any mercury, which is a big drawback to compact fluorescent lights."[4] LED lights also are dimmable and programmable, which meant that Sean potentially had a new palette from which to create the kinds of well- and intelligently lit environments that he was so passionate about.

Soon Sean began to see an opportunity to marry his passion for lighting with his experience in the electronics industry. "I've always wanted to be an entrepreneur," Sean explained, "but with a wife and two kids, I needed the stability and the security that my job provided, especially access to health insurance for my family." But the itch to start a company was too strong for Sean to ignore. He kept his day job but began holding regular Wednesday evening meetings with a potential business partner. And in these after-hours brainstorming sessions, a new company called Alva was born.

The idea behind Alva was to build beautiful architectural lighting fixtures with high-tech LED lights inside them. While the lights would be manufactured offshore, Sean was committed to keeping the higher-paying engineering, design, and sales jobs here in the United States. The lights would consume a fraction of the energy of standard incandescent bulbs, meaning they had a much smaller carbon footprint than most lights. And because they contained no mercury and lasted for decades, Alva's lights virtually eliminated the disposal hazards of compact fluorescent lights. By all accounts, Alva was exactly the sort of company that everyone—from politicians to pundits to environmentalists—seemed to want, one that created good jobs and had positive social and environmental impacts.

So Sean continued to chase his entrepreneurial dreams. He built a prototype, did market research, began to identify sales channels, lined up his supply chain, and landed his first customers, all while continuing to work at his day job. Sean also saved his pennies, in an attempt to self-fund his new venture as much as possible. Along the way he managed to attract a small amount of investment capital; between his own money, his partner's money, and the investor's money, Sean thought he had what he needed to make Alva a reality.

So, on the brink of launching this innovative company, one with all the attributes that everyone seemed to be clamoring for, Sean . . . stopped. He stopped his progress cold and put Alva in a holding pattern. Sean had done everything right. In short order, he had overcome obstacles—idea, product, market, funding, customers—that even the most intelligent, motivated entrepreneurs can't always overcome. And just when everything had fallen into place, Sean hit the barrier that most entrepreneurs never see coming: the inability to afford health insurance for his family. "I knew buying my own insurance for my family was going to be expensive, and I figured I needed about another year's worth of savings in the bank before I was comfortable with this increased financial obligation."

Like most of us in the United States, Sean received health insurance benefits from his employer. These benefits are subsidized in two ways. First, in most states employers that provide health insurance benefits to their employees are required by law to pay for at least part of the premium. Second, these employer-paid premiums aren't treated as taxable income by the Internal Revenue Service, meaning that Uncle Sam does employees the kindness of further subsidizing their (and their family's) health insurance costs. From the insurance companies' perspective, Sean and his family are part of a larger pool of customers, including all the other employees at Sean's company, meaning that the risk of insuring people is spread around, something insurance companies love.

When would-be entrepreneurs step outside this employer-based health insurance system, they lose all these subsidies. Sure, guys like Sean can always buy insurance on the open market, but the system is rigged against them and the premiums are exorbitantly expensive, often putting the option of buying their own insurance out of reach (for the reader's convenience and for the authors' sanity, we will skip the discussion of the major dysfunctions of the American health-care system and why health insurance is so expensive to begin with).

Many entrepreneurs are fortunate that their spouses also work and are able to provide health insurance for the family. This wasn't the case for Sean. His wife—who has a PhD in sociology and does program analysis and evaluation for governments and nonprofits—was also self-employed. She too was "outside the system" and relied on the health insurance benefits that Sean received through his company.

This was the dilemma Sean faced as he stood on the brink of launching his innovative new company. Just to be entirely clear, it's worth reminding ourselves of exactly what this dilemma entails. In Sean we have a smart, motivated entrepreneur with an idea for a great company. The company is going to create good, high-paying jobs in a still-struggling economy. The company is building a product that cuts carbon emissions and is environmentally sustainable. The company is led by an entrepreneur with a passion for his business and for his craft, a passion that will be essential in sustaining the company through the usual ups and downs of any new venture. Most significant, the company has already overcome all the hurdles on the pathway to early success. And the limiting factor in all this has absolutely nothing to do with anything intrinsic to the business. No, the limiting factor is the screwed-up way in which we provide health care and health insurance to each other.

We could use any number of words to describe the dilemma that Sean faced in starting Alva. But here are the ones we like best: *utterly asinine.* Yep, the employer-based system that we use to provide health care and health insurance to each other in this great country of ours, the envy and the economic engine of the world, is just plain silly. And the story of Sean McMurray and his company, Alva, is just one of the millions of representative examples of this silliness.

Plenty of good evidence backs up this claim. The Kauffman Foundation, perhaps the leading organization for advancing entrepreneurship, has teamed with the Rand Corporation to create the Kauffman-Rand Institute for Entrepreneurship Public Policy. In 2010, researchers from the institute published a working paper aptly titled "Is Employer-Based Health Insurance a Barrier to Entrepreneurship?" In the paper, the researchers coin an eloquent—if alarming—phrase: "entrepreneurship lock," the situation that arises when would-be entrepreneurs, like Sean from Alva, get locked into their jobs because of the associated employer-based health insurance benefits and feel forced to delay or forgo the opportunity to start a company. The paper's conclusions are pretty clear: "The potential loss or disruption in health insurance coverage due to pre-existing condition limitations, waiting periods for coverage, changes in health plans and providers, high premiums in the individual health insurance market, and risk of high health costs while uninsured may dissuade many employees from starting a business when it would otherwise be optimal." They go on, in language that economists love, saying that the "bundling of health insurance and employment may create an inefficient allocation of which or when workers start businesses."[5] Markets hate inefficiencies. As a country and as a society, we should be doing everything we possibly can to encourage entrepreneurs like Sean to be able to efficiently come up with new ideas, build companies around those ideas, and create jobs. Perpetuating an arbitrary inefficiency, like employer-sponsored health insurance, into the marketplace for entrepreneurial talent simply doesn't make any sense, particularly as a wider and wider swath of the workforce falls outside the boundaries of traditional employment.

The methodology that the Kauffman-Rand researchers used elegantly captures the negative effect that employer-based health insurance has on entrepreneurship. They studied rates of entrepreneurship and company creation for people in the United States who are just under the age of 65 versus those who are just over the age of 65. For the group just over 65, the researchers found a distinct and statistically significant increase in entrepreneurship. Why? Upon reaching age 65, would-be entrepreneurs are eligible for health insurance through the federal Medicare program, freeing them from the "entrepreneurship lock" of employer-based health insurance. While it's wonderful to know that older Americans are starting companies, it's distressing to think that younger Americans delay or forgo their entrepreneurial aspirations—particularly at a time when our country needs entrepreneurs more than ever—because of their reliance on their employers for something as basic and essential as health insurance.

It's worth reminding ourselves that this system, like so much of what we think of as normal in our economy, is not inevitable. Employer-based health insurance is a mere 60 or 70 years old—not much more than a blip on the 100,000-year time line of human work—and is the result of a historical accident that had a bunch of unintended consequences. Here's what happened: During World War II, the labor market was especially tight because of the all-hands-on-deck war effort. In an attempt to attract workers, companies had to come up with innovative ways to compensate them. One way was to offer employees health insurance. This method of alternative compensation turned out to be pretty popular; powerful labor unions, among other forces, worked hard to institutionalize employer-sponsored health insurance as part of an overall compensation package for workers. Fast-forward a couple of generations and, unless you're poor or old, the only way to get health insurance at a reasonable cost is through your employer.

The evidence in the Kauffman-Rand working paper—not to mention the hundreds of anecdotes we hear from guys like Sean and other NextSpace members—bears out the claim that employer-based health insurance is an enormous hurdle in starting a company and a major inefficiency in the entrepreneurial marketplace. Multiply Sean's story a million times, and we can only conclude that our insistence on perpetuating a system of employer-based health insurance prevents our country, our society, and our economy from operating at its innovative, creative, and productive best. Politicians, policy makers, insurance company executives, and employers are all complicit in perpetuating this arbitrary and inefficient system. To give credit where credit is due, we are hopeful that the recently passed and much debated Affordable Care Act's newly created health exchanges provide a slightly more accessible option, but it may be years before we see whether it is the sort of fundamental change that frees start-ups and small business from entrepreneurship lock.

Our purpose here is not to endorse or offer a bulletproof solution to this problem. Goodness knows, millions of pages of books, reports, studies, and articles have been penned in recent years on the subject of health insurance reform, not to mention thousands of hours of punditry and bloviating on AM radio and cable television. To tread into that debate would be crazy on our part. But we'll just offer this small bit of perspective: health insurance ain't rocket science. An effective insurance system requires that people come together in a risk pool that is as broad and deep as possible and that they pay premiums based on their risk profiles; the insurance company ideally pays out less in claims than it collects in premiums and the government can step in to fill the gaps and ensure the public health and welfare. That's pretty much it. Aggregating people into risk pools based on their employers sure seemed like a good idea at the time, and that idea served us well for decades during an economy that was dominated by steady, long-term employment for most workers.

Now we'll return to one of our favorite stats: according to the *Intuit 2020 Report,* 40 percent of the American workforce won't have employers by 2020.[6] And of those who will have employers, many will be acting as free agents and virtual employees anyway, belonging to a particular company in name only. So in short order there will be no more employees to aggregate into insurance risk pools. Finding a more rational mechanism for aggregating people into risk pools that is reflective of the fact that more and more of us will be working as free agents is an imperative for insurance reform.

We're pretty agnostic about how the government and marketplace will create health insurance risk pools in the future. Maybe we should place people in risk pools based on their zodiac signs. Or based on whether they root for baseball teams in the National League or the American League. Or based on their affinity and tolerance for various reality television shows. These risk pools make about as much sense as pools based on our employers. But this much is essential: once someone has health insurance, that insurance should be portable as that person moves from job to job, gig to gig, or project to project. If that were the case today, Sean McMurray's new company would have been launched an entire year earlier. Sean would have fulfilled his passion and his entrepreneurial dreams that much quicker. He would have created jobs in the midst of a struggling economy. And his company would have helped the environment in a small but significant way. How can we hang on to a system that is directly contradictory to the kind of economy we profess to want and that we so desperately need?

DOUBLE THE TAXATION, DOUBLE THE FUN!

Once an entrepreneur, Smart Generalist, or Super Specialist has made the leap from traditional employment to free agency—presumably finding a way past the health insurance hurdle in the process—a host of additional challenges awaits. The most basic challenge is the effort it takes to get paid. Hustling for work is one thing, but having to track down payments from clients can drive even the most dedicated freelancer to the brink. Freelancers count on getting paid in a timely manner because their income is so variable; sending an invoice to a client and extracting a promise to pay is great, but you can't use that to pay the mortgage.

Shane Pearlman, whom we met in Chapter 1, lamented the difficulties of getting paid by big companies in particular. "When you contract with large companies, they typically pay their vendors on a net 60 basis [meaning that the company can wait as long as 60 days from receipt of an invoice to actually cut a check]. And some of them pay on a net 90 basis. When you're freelancing and sometimes living hand to mouth, two or three months is a long time to wait to get paid."[7] When contracting with smaller companies, many of which have their own cash-flow issues or don't have dedicated accounting departments, tracking down payment can be a nightmare. According to a survey conducted in 2011 by the Freelancers Union, "44 percent of independent workers had trouble getting paid for their work, translating into billions in lost compensation."[8] That's hardly a way to treat 30 to 40 percent of the American workforce.

What's more, freelancers and independent workers aren't given the basic protections that many employees enjoy when it comes to getting paid. When you're an employee and your boss doesn't pay you, you typically have prescribed channels within your company for resolving the issue. At the very least, a mountain of employment law—and state and federal agencies—stands ready to serve you if you need to escalate your claim. No such protections exist for freelancers, who often must immediately resort to litigation. Or, more likely, since litigation can be so expensive and time consuming, they simply forgo getting paid. When 30 to 40 percent of the American workforce has to occasionally forgo getting paid, that's hardly a way to build a healthy, robust economy.

Luckily, technology is helping to relieve this issue. One of our favorite companies, Elance, has created an online platform that includes an escrow system. Freelancers use the system to place their completed work in escrow. And clients place their payments in escrow. Only when both parties have agreed that the work is satisfactorily completed do the work and the money change hands. This system protects clients, ensuring that they receive quality work in accordance with their specifications. And freelancers can be sure that they'll get paid in full in a timely manner. This technology is great, but it's not a substitute for laws and regulations that take into account the unique needs of the freelance and independent workforce.

Perhaps the biggest challenge faced by freelancers is what happens once they actually cash their checks. Before a freelancer does anything with the money—pays rent, buys groceries, pays a babysitter—the first thing she has to do is fork over 15.3 percent (as of this writing) to Uncle Sam. Sure, taxes are a pain, yet most of us accept that taxes are a necessary part of living in civilized society. But this particular tax is especially demoralizing to the freelance and independent workforce. Why? Because this 15.3 percent is a payroll tax, and it's exactly double the amount of payroll tax that people with "real jobs" have to pay.

Here's how it works: We all have to pay payroll taxes. These are taxes that cover Social Security and Medicare. For everyone in the country who collects a paycheck, these taxes are deducted from that paycheck at a standard rate of 15.3 percent (unlike income taxes, which have a sliding rate that depends on how much money you make). Employers are required to pay half that tax on behalf of their employees, meaning only half the tax burden falls on actual employee himself. But if you are self-employed as a freelancer or independent contractor, the government sees you as *both* the employer and the employee, meaning that—whammy!—you're responsible for the entire 15.3 percent.

That, to say the least, is a bummer. In 2012 the US Census Bureau reported that median household income was $50,054 per year. If you earned that money as a freelancer or independent consultant, you pay out of your pocket more than $3,800 per year that your neighbors with "real jobs" don't have to pay. Call us crazy, but that just seems unfair. And, once again, unfairly burdening a large and growing section of the workforce and adversely affecting their productivity and their innovation seems counterproductive to creating a strong economy.

We'll mention only briefly the other policy-related traps and trappings of work that people with "real jobs" don't have to spend a lot of time worrying about. We've already touched on health insurance and taxes, but there's also disability insurance, life insurance, and retirement planning: Roth IRAs, 401(k) s, SEP IRAs, oh my! As an employee with a "real job," your company's human resources department often handles these types of issues. For smaller companies, HR outsourcing companies like TriNet often perform the same function as an in-house HR department.

But when you're a freelancer or independent worker, you *are* the HR department. People in this sector of the workforce can spend enormous chunks of their time navigating the laws and policies that govern work instead of actually performing the work itself. This dilemma cuts down on productivity and innovation, not to mention sanity. As we move forward in the Naked Economy, finding simple, transparent, portable mechanisms for freelancers and independent workers to get the benefits, protections, and fair taxation that they need is of paramount importance. Organizations like Freelancers Union and Elance have made important advances in this effort. Now it's time for politicians and policy makers to step up. Most important, it's time for the 43 million people who make up this sector of the workforce—and whose numbers are growing—to stand up and demand that they be counted.

MAYORS MIGHT SAVE THE WORLD

If the stars align, pigs fly, and hell freezes over, the health insurance, taxes, and benefit mess will be fixed by a polarized and hyperpartisan Congress. If that happens, great. If, more likely, it doesn't, there is still hope. The infrastructure for the Naked Economy will be largely designed, implemented, and modeled by local governments. Cities, small and large, are ground zero for the next economic revolution. The driving forces behind the increasing importance of cities are threefold. First, the world is becoming urbanized. Projections indicate that 70 percent of the world will live in cities by 2050, compared with just over half today and 30 percent in 1950.[9] This will require that cities solve the environmental, social, and economic problems that national governments have thus far failed to address. This urbanization is encouraging a new energy and investment in cities. Around the world we see dynamic mayors, think tanks, and companies imagining how to create a "City 2.0," a concept so important that it won the TED Prize in 2012.[10]

Second, cities have proved themselves to be more entrepreneurial, more willing to take risks, and more eager to test new ideas. Among the more prominent examples are mayors signing on to regional climate change compacts in the absence of international action, and new initiatives like Michael Bloomberg's $9 million prize for innovative cities, Google's city broadband competition, or Code for America's efforts to improve cities' use of technology. All these efforts demonstrate that capital and ideas are not willing to persist in using the byzantine machinery of state and national governments to make change. In a world where money, ideas, and attention move at the speed of a tweet, the city may be only the governmental entity capable of keeping up.

The third force is one that has been demonstrated by nearly everyone in this book, from Shane, who surfs in Santa Cruz, to Ben, who lives with his family in Iowa, to the WordPress editor, who decided she wanted to try living in Vietnam for a couple of months: we are moving toward an economy in which people can live and work where they choose. This is one of the biggest benefits of the Naked Economy. The workplace is location neutral. Talent in this century will flow not only among countries but among cities, neighborhoods, coffee shops, and coworking spaces. As we mentioned in Chapter 6, Matt Mullenweg of Automattic reminds us that workers now "can arbitrage their lives."

For cities this reality will be a profound change. Cities have traditionally been formed around industries and companies. Economic development meant attracting and retaining companies with tax breaks, ribbon cuttings, and infrastructure projects. City planning assumed that the community would be divided into neat districts where citizens would work (high rises and factories), shop (malls), and live (neighborhoods). Even the advent of the "new urbanism," designs to make cities more livable, simply adjusted the old paradigm to put these uses into walkable neighborhoods. Now these uses may occur in the same apartment.

The old model of building cities around employers missed the point. It wasn't the companies that the city wanted, it was the jobs. The company just happened to be the container in which those jobs were delivered. But as the workforce continues to disaggregate, the company is no longer the most efficient way to bring jobs to a community. Remember the story of how we came up with NextSpace. We, as mayor and economic development manager, got tired of romancing companies to move to Santa Cruz by one-upping other towns' offers of tax breaks and subsidies. Instead we looked around our coffee shops and saw the hundreds of people tapping away on their laptops and conducting business on their smart phones. These members of the disaggregated workforce were a major force in our local economy, mimicking the high-paying creative jobs that we so desperately wanted to attract. But we realized that no one was paying attention to this group at all, even though it represented our best hope for economic development. So we realized that instead of attracting one 200-person company, we should build space for 200 one-person companies. The 200-person company could go out of business, pick up and move away, or spend years negotiating tax breaks and land acquisitions. Those one-person companies had already chosen Santa Cruz and were building their lives here. These people were going to spend their money at our local businesses, send their kids to our local schools, and volunteer at our local civic organizations. We don't need their employers, especially when we already have the employees.

Edward Glaeser, a leader in the study of economics and cities, observed, "The future of most cities depends on there being desirable places for consumers to live. As consumers become richer and firms become mobile, location choices are based as much on their advantages for workers as on their advantages for firms."[11] As cities shift from designing themselves around companies to around their citizens, there will be an incredible opportunity to reinvent, reinvest, and reimagine the city. New approaches to zoning, open space, taxes, and the safety net will determine which cities attract and retain the talent around which their economies will flourish. Local governments will be a responsive and integral partner in the emerging economy. As Richard Florida wrote in *Rise of the Creative Class,* "The bottom line is that cities need a people climate as much as and perhaps even more than, they need a business climate."[12]

SMALL BUSINESS IS BIG

While the need for new policies is large, the focus of public policy has to be small—very small. Government will have to be a platform for, as well as partner and encourager of, microbusinesses. Freelancers, contractors, and one-person companies are not only the wave of the future, they are also the overwhelming majority of current economic activity. Jim Clifton, CEO of Gallup, notes that "as of 2007, there were about 6 million businesses in the United States with at least one employee; businesses with 500 or fewer employees represent more then 99 percent of these 6 million."[13]

Nonetheless, if you walk into the Small Business Administration, local economic development office, or even a bank and say, "Hi, I'm a one-person contractor. What can you do to support me?" you will get blank stares, if not a polite walk out the door. Government programs and private capital are not structured to work in the new economy because they have been able to take the easy route with the large employers. Yet one could easily argue that a small loan—often in the neighborhood of, say, $10,000—to that contractor and tens of thousands like her would have a greater economic impact (not to mention likelihood of being paid back) than the bailout of a big Wall Street bank or insurance company.

Small businesses win not only in terms of quantity but quality. Edward Glaeser and William Kerr reported in "The Secret to Job Growth: Think Small" that regional economic growth is highly correlated with the presence of many small entrepreneurial employers—not a few big ones. In fact, a study of US metro regions showed that cities whose number of firms per worker was 10 percent higher than the average in 1977 experienced 9 percent faster employment growth between 1977 and 2000.[14]

In the NextSpace ecosystem or a Mumbai neighborhood, the clustering of entrepreneurs generates opportunity. Policies that support (or at the very least don't hinder) increasing the number of single-person firms, like Mike Farmer's mobile app company, are the key to our future. As Richard Adler wrote for the Aspen Institute in 2011, "An agency like the Small Business Administration works on the assumption that every small business intends to grow into a large business and does not recognize the potential of network effects that can be generated by the creative collaboration of many small enterprises."[15]

BETTER TOGETHER

What do tech giants Google and Amazon have in common with Ben & Jerry's and Build-a-Bear Workshop? These companies, among thousands of others, allow and encourage employees to bring their dogs to work. Dog-friendly companies often say that employee recruitment and retention is the reason behind allowing pooches in the workplace. Even better, bringing Fido to work can make employees more productive and collaborative. The Humane Society of the United States cites a 2010 study conducted by Central Michigan University, which found "that when dogs were present in a group, employees were more likely to trust each other and collaborate more effectively in the office." A senior official at the Human Society lauded the study's conclusions, saying, "We heartily agree with the positive impact that dogs can have on workplace morale, collaboration, and productivity."[16] To our ears, more trust, collaboration, and productivity in the workplace seems like the perfect recipe for success in the Naked Economy.

Diana Rothschild has spent the last couple of years thinking about how to achieve personal and professional productivity and sustainability. Like many of the people that we've met in this book, Diana has a pretty enviable resumé. She holds an undergraduate degree from the Haas School of Business at University of California Berkeley and an MBA from Stanford. As a buyer and supply planner for Walmart, she helped create and implement Walmart's sustainability programs. From that experience, Diana became an in-demand consultant to Fortune 100 companies, often tagging along on corporate jets as she advised CEOs on how to make their companies' products, services, and business models more sustainable. Then Diana did what lots of women in their twenties and thirties do: she had a baby, a beautiful daughter that quickly became the focus of Diana's, and her husband Gabe's, lives. "I've always believed in sustainability, in all of its forms," Diana says, "but when I had my daughter, I had a renewed perspective on why we even bother with sustainability and who we're sustaining things for."[17]

Of course, having a child forced Diana and her husband to rethink how they balance work and family. Diana knew she wanted to return to work in some capacity sometime during her daughter's first year. But she also knew that she needed to return to work on terms that would allow her to more closely integrate being a mom with being a high-flying member of the corporate world. During her maternity leave, Diana and her daughter often spent time at parks and playgrounds near their home in San Francisco. While the kids played, Diana met other moms and dads who were facing the same dilemma of balancing work and family. Like Diana, many of these parents were smart, educated, successful people who had been doing important, meaningful work before having kids. However, feeling like they couldn't strike a successful balance—in fact, feeling like the System was rigged against such balance—many of these parents had simply decided to drop out of the workforce all together, typically opting to take four or five years off to raise their kids until the kids were old enough to go to school.

"I'm well aware of the mommy wars," Diana explains, "and I absolutely respect any parent's decision to stay home with their kids. But I was struck by how many parents felt that staying home was the only choice. And I would look at these parents, these amazing people with PhDs and MBAs and incredible skills and experience, and think to myself, 'Wait! The world needs you! We've got too many challenges and too many opportunities in front of us as a country, as a society, and as a planet for you to be sitting on the sidelines for the next four or five years.' So I began to think that there must be a way for people to be able to work productively while still being present as parents." To put it another way: if bringing your dog to work can make you more productive, shouldn't there be a way to boost your productivity and happiness by bringing your kid to work?

With this idea in mind, Diana founded NextKids, a collaborative space that combines professional workspace, supportive community, and a first-rate child-care space. Diana's philosophy is remarkably simple and echoes the anthropology that we've covered in others parts of this book: parents and children are better together. We evolved as a species to work, live, and play in proximity to each other. By separating the act of "working" with the act of "parenting," we remove the opportunity for both parents and children to work—yes, play is work!—at their creative, productive, and innovative best. By bringing "working" and "parenting" back together, both parents and children can thrive together, equally and without compromise. "In observing parents trying to strike that all-important balance between work and family," Diana says, "I discovered that what the world most needs is for all of us to bring our whole selves to work and life every day. What better way to play our biggest game than to do it with the ones we love most, the way we were meant to: together."

Over the past few decades, the System has created ways to make the separation from our kids more palatable. While programs like the Family Medical Leave Act, Paid Family Leave, child-care tax credits, and required dedicated rooms for nursing mothers offer financial and temporary job security, they don't celebrate Diana's philosophy of fully integrating work and family. Nearly a third of Fortune's 2012 "100 Best Companies to Work For" offer onsite childcare centers.[18] These corporations see this benefit as a critical way to attract and retain top talent and increase productivity. These centers immediately have long waitlists and complicated lottery systems for enrollment and some are building even larger care centers to meet expected needs in 5–10 years; soon enough, the companies' talented twenty-somethings will be ready for kids and companies won't want to lose that talent to rival firms. While these policies are great solutions for the corporate parent, parents who are part of the freelance and independent workforce don't always have good options for childcare. Using the real-time workplace framework that we developed in Chapter 8, Diana's idea for NextKids gives these parents the location, infrastructure, and vibe they need to work at their creative, productive, and innovative best. Diana thinks of it like this: "If taking your dog to work can increase your productivity and sense of well-being, imagine how much more happy, productive, and focused you'd be knowing that, while you're on that all-important conference call or cranking out a high-priority report, your child was being well cared for in the next room. And imagine that your reward for closing that deal or delivering that report was a smile and a hug from the most important person on Earth. Ultimately, isn't that why we work in the first place?"

READING, WRITING, ENTREPRENEURSHIP

One final policy area needs to be developed for the Naked Economy—teaching entrepreneurship. The economic, cultural, and technological changes to the economy require that workers be, if not entrepreneurs, at least entrepreneurial. Yet, when we look at the skills we offer the next generation in our schools, entrepreneurship is nearly nonexistent in K–12 curriculums and mostly an elective for college business majors. For many their childhood experience of running a lemonade stand has been their most intensive training. Organizations like the Kauffman and Skoll foundations are beginning to shift the debate, but there is a long way to go.

It will not be enough for the Super Specialists of the future to rely on their single expertise. They will need to know just enough about marketing, finance, and strategy to translate their skills into a living. Even those who will work for large companies are going to be expected to be entrepreneurial in their work as they navigate their way through the corporate maze. Reid Hoffman, founder of LinkedIn, calls this "The Start-up of You." In his book by that title he and coauthor Ben Casnocha write, "What's required now is an entrepreneurial mind-set. Whether you work for a ten-person company, a giant multinational corporation, a not-for-profit, a government agency, or any type of organization in between—if you want to seize the new opportunities and meet the challenges of today's fractured career landscape, you need to think and act like you're running a start-up: your career."[19]

The mind-set and skills required to think this way do not come naturally. Our current educational system, designed for the industrial era, is not structured to provide the culture and training that encourage entrepreneurial thinking. The good news is that entrepreneurship training is in demand. A 2006 poll of 1,474 middle and high school students by the youth entrepreneurship organization Junior Achievement found that

70.9 percent would like to be self-employed at some point in their lives. That was up from 68.6 percent in 2005 and 64 percent in 2004, according to *Businessweek*.[20] Now schools need to develop platforms that allow students to develop their ideas, work in teams, and gain the skills that are required for our economy.

However, in the new economy education will not end with a diploma. The constant acquisition of skills and knowledge will be a requirement for every worker. In "Working Nonstop to Stay Relevant," the *New York Times* noted that with continuous advances in technology, everyone from car mechanics to PhD computer scientists must constantly train and adapt and do so on their own time and dime.[21]

"Whether you want to learn a new skill or simply be better at the job you were hired to do, it's now your job to train and invest in yourself," Hoffman and Casnocha explain.[22] Companies don't want to invest in you, in part because you're not likely to commit years and years of your life to working for them—you will have many different jobs in your lifetime. As we have already seen, there used to be a long-term pact between employee and employer that guaranteed lifelong employment in exchange for lifetime loyalty; we've also seen lots of examples of how this pact has been replaced by performance-based, short-term contracts that are perpetually up for renewal on both sides. Professional loyalty now flows horizontally—to and from your network rather than vertically to your boss.

The new platforms for training, education, and research need to be broad based, open to all, and implemented soon. "We need to get beyond the notion that innovation is something that only occurs among scientists and more often than not it comes from small things," Richard Florida argues. "We need to see all members of society as potential innovators, stoke their innovative potential, and extend the definition of innovation beyond technology and R&D to include investment in the arts, in culture, and in every other form of creativity." Or, as the former Intel CEO Andy Grove, asked: "What kind of society are we going to have, if it consists of highly paid people doing high-value-added work—and mass unemployment?"[23]

PART IV

CONCLUSION

CHAPTER 10

WHAT TO EXPECT WHEN YOU'RE EXPECTING THE NAKED ECONOMY

A lot of people refuse to do things because they don't want to go naked, don't want to go without guarantee. But that's what's got to happen. You go naked until you die.

—Nikki Giovanni

NAVIGATING NAKEDNESS

Throughout this book we've explored the causes and effects of the economic revolution we are experiencing and have visited people who have survived the bumpy ride from one economic model to another. Iowan Ben Gran, you'll remember, went from panic attacks in his 9-to-5 cubicle to a freelancing career that allows him to work with clients all over the world. Sandy Skees was once threatened with termination if she ever missed a meeting because of child-care problems. Now, as a public relations executive and entrepreneur, she's in a position to help other women negotiate the tricky calculus of family and career. We've met enlightened companies like the employee-owned

New Belgium Brewing Company, and Philip Rosedale, who figured out a way for workers to set each other's salaries. And we've met capable and industrious middle-class Americans who have found a way to do what they love—like Wallace "J." Nichols, who defied the hidebound practices of academia to popularize saving the sea turtle, and Shane Pearlman, who, despite having been laid off five times, has found a way to make his livelihood conform to his values and not the other way around.

For these brave pioneers, the road has sometimes been bumpy because the rules of the old economy are often diametrically opposed to the kind of living and the kind of life that they're trying to build. The upshot is, yes, your grandfather's economy, your mother's economy—even your older sister's economy—is collapsing because the rules that governed it no longer make sense. The result of that collapse is not merely chaotic wreckage—though, understandably, it can look and feel that way to many—but an understructure of opportunity and a chance to bring different values to the workplace. A naked economy, like being naked, can be scary, but it can also lead to some of the best moments in one's life.

So whether you're the midcareer professional who still believes that your work life should be better than it is, or a laid-off tech worker with a good idea and a lot of contacts that can help you make it happen, or a 30-something worker trying to figure out how to advance professionally while still seeing your family, or the recent college grad who finds yourself in the jungle of the modern labor force without a map and bug spray, the new economy has a lot of opportunity. But how do you find the prosperity that you are looking for?

Everyone needs to find their own path, but from our dozens of interviews and watching thousands of independent workers in NextSpace navigate the new economy, we've put together five hints—all mutually reinforcing—that should help you move into the Naked Economy.

1. FIND YOUR OWN TURTLES

Heather Stephenson digs what she calls "light-green living." She's not talking about living off the grid in the hills but rather about being part of that growing community of sophisticated connected folks who are passionate about living with a small carbon footprint. As Heather put it, "We're crafters, foodies, DIYers, and the kind of people who have chickens in their backyard."

Heather runs a company called The Old School (theold-school.com), which develops online tools and access points for folks looking to break away from rampant consumerism and take more control of their own lives, "whether it's curing your own sausage or making your own limoncello." Her site offers tips and lessons by e-mail, social media, or smart-phone apps and allows people to pursue online or offline classes in everything from letterpress printing to quilting.

This is not Heather's first venture in which she has drawn on her interests and passions to build a business. She has started up websites and digital media companies in a number of settings, from the urban dynamism of Brooklyn to the wide-open spaces of Montana. She has worked for big companies. In fact, she was a part of the vast Disney empire for a while. But she's always gone back to working on her own, finding a way to blend the need for making a living with a need for letting her passions guide her.

"I always get to be around the people I want to be working with," she said about the positives of hanging out your own shingle. "Surrounding myself with like-minded people who inspire me and bring their own passions to the party, so to speak, is a big part of why I do what I do. Flexibility of my time is really second to that."

Just out of college, with a mind to make television commercials and print ads, she got a job with an advertising company and worked on creating online advertising, which, in 1995 was a brave new frontier. At 27 she had become adept enough at it that she was sent to London to run another start up's European branch. "That gave me a taste of what it was like to be independent and to be in charge of my own business, even though it was part of the bigger company."

She soon left that company to branch out on her own and tap into her passion for sustainable living, establishing a website called Ideal Bite, a lifestyle site for green living that targeted an affluent, mostly female, audience. The site grew from 300 friends and family members to more than a half-million subscribers. Three years later, in 2008, the Walt Disney Company purchased the site, and, as part of the deal, Heather and her business partner were brought under Disney's enormous umbrella as employees.

The allure of flying solo, however, led her to break out on her own again, this time by establishing The Old School. On the side, Heather has also produced apps in the health-and-wellness arena that are specifically aimed at yoga practitioners. "Ideal Bite gave me a heady taste of doing well by doing good. Living my passion is really addicting. Knowing that what you're doing can both help you make a living and do something good for the planet is hard to give up, and it's hard to move away from that once you have it."

At 39 Heather is a kind of expert in a realm in which there were no experts just a decade ago. Online media are an ever-evolving world, she said, and it still has opportunities for those with the moxie to take a risk.

> One of the things that confounds a lot of people is that they feel like they're faking it. Everything moves so quickly in digital media. Whenever there's a new thing that no one is an expert in yet, people think that they're faking it when they work in that area. The thing is, everybody, even the most seasoned professionals, feels like they're faking it when it comes to these new business models and technologies. So the advice I would give is to kind of fake it until you do become an expert in whatever you're doing. By the time that happens, there's something new that you'll be faking. And by "faking," I don't mean positioning yourself in some kind of untrue way. I mean following your passion and figuring things out as you go, acting as if you've got a least a few of the answers, if not all of them. Someone has to decide how social media is going to make money. Someone has to figure out new business models that allow people make a living while helping people and the planet. It might as well be you. So following your passion, picking up the banner and running with it, sometimes works out really well.[1]

2. KEEP YOUR COSTS LOW, YOUR DISCIPLINE STRONG, AND YOUR HAPPINESS HIGH

The new economy that is freeing many workers from the dictates of time (9-to-5) and space (the office cubicle) is also rewriting the concepts of industrial management that have been in place for more than 100 years. The Quaker-born Pennsylvanian Frederick Winslow Taylor (1856–1915) is credited as the father of modern management, and among his many ideas that shaped the structure and culture of the modern office was that workers naturally want to avoid work and thus must be closely supervised. You could argue, in fact, that the central purpose of the traditional office is, and always has been, management supervision. This notion has been heeded ferociously for decades. But, as we explored in Chapter 8, the huge surge in mobility, the growing irrelevance of the modern office, and the rise of the workplace ecosystem are hallmarks of work life today. Suddenly, Taylor's watch-them-like-a-hawk belief system is not only totally out of date but also not productive.

In 2002 Zach Hochstadt and his business partner Jennie Winton founded Mission Minded, a marketing, strategy, and branding firm that works exclusively with nonprofits. The company has never had a physical office. "Ten years ago there was something novel about what we were doing," Zach said. "But it was simple economics that made us decide not to invest in an office. Jennie and I worked for an employer who had gone under, in part because he had expensive real estate he had to keep up. We said to ourselves, 'We don't want to be there.'"

Mission Minded's clientele includes a wide variety of nonprofits, from the San Francisco Opera to the Denver Art Museum to the San Francisco AIDS Foundation. Working with nonprofits, whose budgets are often a fraction of what private-sector clients might pay, means that Mission Minded needs to run a lean operation, forgoing the office and related overhead expenses. Today the company employs about 25 people, some of them full-time salaried employees and the rest contractors, all of whom work remotely. In the early days Zach didn't let on to potential clients that his company didn't have a physical address. "We didn't make a big deal out of the fact that we didn't have an office. Usually we would just meet our clients in their office spaces. That solution seemed to satisfy many of the folks that we wanted to work with." A nice bonus: every dollar not spent on overhead means Zach has greater capacity to serve nonprofits that often lack the same budgets as the for profit sector.

Keeping costs low also means taking advantage of free or inexpensive means of production—the stuff you need to make your business go—for the kinds of tasks most people are doing in the Naked Economy. Need some software? There's probably a free open-source version or an inexpensive web-based version that'll meet your needs. Need an extra set of hands when things get busy? Don't hire an employee, simply take a spin through Task Rabbit or Mechanical Turk to find exactly the skills you need in exactly the dose that you need them. Travel costs seem too high? A Zipcar and an Airbnb reservation let you travel in style for very little cash. Need to find a place to hold a meeting with that all-star client? LiquidSpace has got you covered. The sharing economy, estimated to be a $110 billion market by 2012, and the ethos of access versus ownership are not only ways to get our hands on the things we need to be productive; they also strengthen the social capital required to glue the Naked Economy together.[2]

Still, all this freedom means we have to be hypervigilant about staying productive and maintaining some boundaries between the various facets of our lives. Zach runs his business from his Denver home, but his mind-set keeps work and life distinct. After all, there's something to old Frederick Winslow Taylor's assertion that unwatched workers will tend to goof off.

So Zach has created a set of simple rites and rituals to keep him motivated when no one is around to crack the whip. "I'm really disciplined about my transitions from home mode to work mode," he said. "I make sure to shower every morning and get dressed for work, even though work is only 20 feet away. It seems simple, but it helps me make that transition."

Zach and Jennie have also created the ritual of the 9 A.M. phone call. Every morning they jump on a quick call together. There's never much of an agenda, just a chance to say hello and see what's on each other's mind for the day. Most important, the phone call is designed to enforce a sense of discipline and keep each other accountable.

Of course one side effect of shrugging off the corporate overload is that we no longer have anyone to tell us when *not* to work. For driven, motivated entrepreneurs like Zach, the temptation to work all the time can be pretty strong. "One of the challenges we're seeing today," Zach said, "is that people never stop working. We're always connected. We're always up. We're always on. For me it's a big benefit to say OK, I've learned the disciplines of how to be at home or how to be at work, to develop a mind-set for each, and to feel like I've re-created some separation between the two."

So Zach applies the same discipline to stop working that he does to start working. "I end work at a set time every day," Zach said. "I never just keep working, working, working. I have a family and child-rearing responsibilities. So I have that stop time, which means I need to get my work done in the time available. And that helps me transition when I leave my 'office' and I come 'home.'"[3]

In the 1990s and early 2000s, much of the debate about the balance between working and leisure focused on drawing the boundaries between the two even more dramatically. The development of the smart phone and ubiquitous, always-on connectivity created new breaches in that boundary. Dreamy anecdotes of taking a quick business call or checking e-mail while lounging on the beach morphed into nightmare visions of a generation worried that the constant demands of their jobs would swallow them.

To combat this anxiety companies like Volkswagen are experimenting with turning off their employees' access to e-mail after they leave work until they come in the next morning. Boston Consulting Group is coordinating agreements to give its high-powered and highly stressed consultants nights off from their cell phones. Leslie Purlow, a Harvard Business School professor who conducted the research for Boston Consulting Group, was initially surprised by the reaction that the consultant had to the experiment: "Some said they didn't know what they would do with a night off," she said.[4] But eventually the consultant realized that having the discipline to turn off and unplug made them more productive at their jobs, more satisfied with their work, and happier with their lives.

The discipline to create balance in your life is an absolutely essential skill in the Naked Economy. Study after study has found that a balanced life—including sleep, physical activity, interests outside work, and a chance to engage in that age-old pursuit of happiness—leads to more productivity. Happiness has become such a core metric for company success that the *Harvard Business Review* made it a central theme of its January 2012 issue. In the issue's introduction, the editors use some pretty bold language to describe the impact of happiness on productivity: "Emerging research from neuroscience, psychology, and economics makes the link between a thriving workforce and better business performance absolutely clear. Happiness can have an impact at both the company and the country level. And the movement to measure national well-being on factors other than GDP could be game changing. . . . We've learned a lot about how to make people happy. We'd be stupid not to use that knowledge."

3. WORK YOUR NETWORK, GET OUT OF YOUR HOUSE, AND FIND YOUR TRIBE

Donnie Fowler has built an impressive dual career in politics and high tech. He has worked as a national staffer on every Democratic presidential campaign since 1988, including serving as the national field and delegates director for Al Gore's 2000 campaign. During Bill Clinton's second term, Donnie served as a presidential appointee at the Federal Communications Commission and was in the agency during the dot-com boom of the 1990s. After the 2000 election, he came to Silicon Valley to build bridges between the high-tech industry and policy makers.

Donnie is an example of a midcareer worker who has found a niche built largely on his Rolodex. He has adopted the Hollywood model—along with our Generalist-Specialist model—of bringing together a collection of talented people to fill roles for a specific period of time to bring a single project to fruition. After landing a contract to deliver a certain project in a certain time frame, he goes on the hunt for professionals to build his team. "I have a long list of talent to draw from," he said, "a deep bench, you might say. Even if the first person I go to is not available, I've got three or four people I can go to without any problem. If I can't get Brad Pitt, instead of waiting for him to be available, I can go get George Clooney or Matt Damon."

Your guess is as good as ours as to whether Donnie is speaking metaphorically here.

When the trappings of employment change radically—when a steady paycheck, corner office, receptionist, and dedicated parking space all disappear—the most valuable things that people midcareer are left with are their experiences and their relationships, both personal and professional. For workers who have spent years developing these contacts, working on your own doesn't have to diminish those relationships. For take-charge personalities who can live without the security of a steady paycheck, the traditional corporate structure is just one more accessory that you can do without.

"Being on your own is feast or famine," Donnie said. "When gigs are lean, I'm not paying a bunch employees who don't have a lot of work to do or servicing a lot of corporate overhead. And when I do have projects, I'm actually able to go get some more senior people with broader or deeper experience and bring them into that project. For example, let's take a national project for clean energy for different states around the country. I could have had three or four 25-year-olds that have some clean-energy or campaign experience. Or I could have four people who have very senior, national-level experience on the issues. Either way, when that project ends, so does my commitment and obligation to pay them."

Donnie is the first to admit, however, that his approach may not apply to everyone in the workforce, particularly those fresh out of college. "I don't think I could pull this off if I was just getting into the workforce," he said. "Because of the substantive knowledge I've gained and the number of relationships I've built, my network is pretty deep and broad. That's hard to mimic when you're just starting out."[5] But one thing's for certain: you won't find your network by sitting alone in your house.

Indeed this need to get out, to connect, and to interact with other people is what drives many independent workers to hang out at coffee shops, coworking spaces, and other "third places." Initially they may not be looking to form strong networks. Instead they're simply driven by this deeply human need to be social and to be around other people. But when they do venture out, and when they do so intentionally, they often find that the world is full of people who have the kinds of skills that can help move a project forward. More broadly, these independent workers often find that they can tap into a much wider group of people with complementary skills sets and different perspectives. Donnie's network is a good example of these stronger connections. These wider, weaker connections have several names, but here's the one we like best: *the tribe*.

Independent workers need the strong ties that come from being plugged into a network. These strong ties provide expertise, camaraderie, and trusted advice. But they also need the weak ties that come from being part of a larger tribe: people who are enough like us that we can recognize them as friends and not foes but who are different enough from us to provide new insights, broader perspectives, and news from complementary industries. Practically speaking, these weak ties are often the way that independent workers land new gigs, gain new skills, or find new ways to ply their trade. To paraphrase Xavier de Souza Briggs, an MIT professor known for his work on the power of social capital: networks are useful for *getting by;* tribes are useful for *getting ahead.*

Spencer Lindsay, a digital artist and the sole proprietor of Lindsay Digital, uses the power of his tribe to make his business more successful. After years of working alone out of his garage, Spencer became a member of NextSpace in 2011. He noted that his productivity has increased as a result of having other interesting creative people working nearby. "But what I really need," said Spencer with some enthusiasm, "are all the other things that make my business go: bookkeeping, billing, invoicing, taxes, legal compliance. I'm an artist and I suck at that stuff! You can read a million how-to books, but it's easier and more effective to meet someone while grabbing a cup of coffee, find out that they have the skills that I need, and let them take care it. Then I get back to doing what I do well: making cool digital pictures for video games, museum displays, architects, and designers."[6] Judging by his work—he recently received national recognition for 3D renderings of phytoplankton for a display at the Monterey Bay Aquarium—Spencer's tribe is definitely helping him get ahead in the Naked Economy.

4. GET OUT OF YOUR HEAD

Tess Finnegan is in her late thirties and the mother of three children, all younger than seven. She spends a good part of her day doing the things that lots of moms do: making sure everyone is clothed and fed, off to school, and back home. She hopes to have enough time left over to sit on the floor and play dolls with her daughter for a few minutes. Tess also makes time to take a few yoga classes every week. "They're good for my sanity," she said with a laugh. Her husband, Laurent, is a vice president for global asset management for a major hotel chain and, for now, the family's primary breadwinner.

That wasn't always the case. Tess has the academic credentials and resumé to win more than her fair share of bread. She has an undergraduate degree from Princeton and a law degree from American University. She worked as an associate at a high-flying law firm in Washington, DC, then spent several years at the US Department of Justice working behind the scenes on a number of very public cases. "I can't really talk about the details," Tess said with a sly smile.

She stepped away from all that when she realized that trying to balance a high-powered career with raising young children did not satisfy her. "The kids are only young once," she said. "As their mom, you have the rare privilege of getting to view the world through the eyes of your children. That privilege lasts only a few years and I didn't want to miss it."

Tess has been away from her career for almost five years and has no regrets. Still, she feels the inexorable tug of the work world. "There's so much interesting stuff happening these days at the intersection of technology, mobility, policy, and communication. I definitely want to be a part of that, but in a way that allows me to stay true to my desire to be a major presence in my kids' childhood."

Inspired by other people—mostly other moms—who are creating success in this new reality of blending work and family, Tess is in the early stages of launching a new company. The company is building a mobile application that augments and enhances the tourist experience in Washington, DC, and ("Someday!" she said) other cities around the world. "So many families come to DC for that once-in-a-lifetime vacation to our nation's capital. There's so much to do and see, so many interesting and little-known details about our country's history and our government. I want people to be able to access all of that information during their visits."

Of course, building a company is no small feat under any circumstances, particularly when you're also trying to raise a pack of kids. The pressure—generated both internally by a smart, driven woman who is accustomed to success and externally by a society that tells her, quite overtly, that success is her only option—can quickly become crippling. "I had to get out of my head," Tess explained. "I had to find a way to ignore the noise and combat some of the fear and anxiety. Mostly, I wanted to be able to connect with other people who were doing interesting things to create value in the world, leading sane, sustainable lives, and redefining success on their own terms."

Tess took a simple, elegant approach to solving this problem. She created a "personal board of directors." Much like a company's board of directors, Tess's personal board provides strategic guidance, forges useful connections, and keeps her accountable to her goals. Her board includes other entrepreneurs—a teacher who now owns her own yoga studio and a woman who started a successful real estate staging company—as well as more established business people, such as the CEO of an educational technology company. She also has a few people on her board purely to provide motivation, like the guy she knows from high school who constantly posts inspirational photos and poetry on his Facebook page. For Tess, the value of her board boils down to this: "When you're trying to redefine success on your own terms, it's easy to listen to the naysayers in your head. It's easy to get stuck seeing only the barriers. More than anything, my board helps me focus on the possibilities instead of on the barriers."

What might that success look like, both for Tess and for the rest of us as we begin to transition to the Naked Economy? For

Tess the key words are *balance* and *choice.* "Like everyone else, I have the same 24 hours in my day. I get to choose how to spend that time as I balance my desire to be a great mom and my desire to create an interesting, valuable product. Approaching that choice with purpose and intention—and getting feedback and validation on that choice from my board—makes everything seem a little less scary and a little more doable. That's incredibly empowering."[7]

5. REMEMBER WHY YOU WORK

Alas, the workforce is not made entirely of tech entrepreneurs running businesses from a laptop at a coffee shop or coworking space. If the Naked Economy works for them, it's going to have to work for the rest of us as well. So it's worth taking a moment—once we strip away the office cube farm, smart phone, health insurance and 401(k) benefits, long commutes, even longer work hours, and the accompanying anxiety that seems to pervade everything—to reflect on why, exactly, we work in the first place. For most of us the goal is simple, although many of us have forgotten how simple it really is: we work to earn a living and to feed, clothe, and shelter ourselves and our families; we work to create something meaningful and valuable in the world; and we work to leave a legacy, through the things we make, the impacts we have, and, perhaps most important, the children that we leave behind. Think about it: creatures are born, grab a meal, find a mate, create some offspring, and then die. They exist, often terribly briefly, for the sole purpose of leaving a legacy. Are we so very different?

The challenge for us higher-order beings is to find a way to intentionally and artfully blend the here and now of making a living with our desire to create meaning and value and leave a legacy. Not an easy task, and it's made even harder because our collective social contract is no longer relevant, and the policies that govern our social structures, as we've seen, have yet to adapt to that change.

Independent workers—the kind that we've met throughout this book—deal with this challenge most acutely. Our friend Heather, despite the success of following her passion and creating The Old School, still has to figure out how to sustain this success while taking care of her most important legacy-creating activity: taking care of her daughter. Working moms need child care not just so they can physically go to another place to perform their duties as a worker. Even if you're at home, it can be hard to have time to focus and feel professional when the kids are running around like crazy.

Heather has a part-time nanny who looks after her daughter and another child in her home while she's working. "Everything in my life has to be very structured because I have child care three days a week," she said. "There are absolute set times that I have to schedule meetings, take conference calls, do lunch appointments, and those times fill up fast." Work-at-home parents have challenges that go-to-the-office parents don't have. At home a parent's physical absence ideally means they are at work. But when a parent is working from home, they have to develop structures to ensure that their children understand when the parent is at work and when she isn't. "I never want her to feel that she's competing with my phone or my computer," Heather said of her young daughter, "and it's really challenging to compartmentalize that part of my life. When she comes back from the park, I'll spend some time with her, I'll play with her, I'll make her some lunch and then go back to work. That's a huge benefit for both of us. But she does see me staring at a screen a lot, and I don't want her thinking that's all there is to the world."

So Wednesdays are devoted entirely to her daughter. These days, particularly with long-standing clients, such habits are understood to be a normal part of a working mother's life. But, she acknowledges, when dealing with larger corporate clients, she still has to tell little white lies about why she's not available on Wednesday. Heather simply says she has meetings all day Wednesday, conveniently leaving out that those meetings are with a 13-month-old ball of energy. "Really, they're my most important meetings of the week." Transitioning to a whole new work environment means Heather can make those all-important meetings for a long time to come.

Not everyone in the Naked Economy is raising children. But creating value and meaning and leaving a legacy can take many forms. Nafeesa Monroe does not have to worry about children, but she has a different passion that she balances with her need to make a living: her art. She's learned to skillfully tailor a lifestyle that allows her to earn some money and still create the art she loves, although not necessarily at the same time.

Nafeesa is an actor. And like legions of actors before her, she moved to Los Angeles to pursue her career and kept food on the table by serving it to others. That old cliché, that every server is an actor waiting for the big break, turned out to be true in Nafeesa's case. "That's what actors in LA do," she said, "because that's how you maintain your flexibility to go to auditions." But after a year of waiting tables, she decided that she "absolutely hated it." And, given that she wasn't exactly being overwhelmed with offers to act, she had to figure out something else to do.

Nafeesa also has a background in science and math. She attended Wesleyan University, got a degree in math, and earned a fellowship that landed her at the NASA Ames Research Center in Mountain View, California. So when she grew tired of waiting tables in LA, she had some pretty impressive credentials to fall back on. "One day I'm on Craigslist," she said, "when I saw a listing looking for SAT tutors in math. I had tutored a 12-year-old girl once, and I felt it was something that I was good at." So she signed up with a tutoring service.

She was pleasantly surprised to find that the service, as well as the families that subscribe to the service, like the idea of actors as tutors. "Actors make really good tutors and teachers," she said. "We're engaging. We're funny. And if we're smart enough to do the work and teach the kids, it's a win-win situation. We also have the flexibility in our schedules to meet kids after school or on the weekends."

The job was a nice fit with her passion for acting, and Nafeesa has been earning a living as a part-time worker for a company that supplies SAT tutors as well as through her own company, Be Superb. It's a gig that allows her to still have the flexibility to go to auditions, rehearsals, and performances. And new inexpensive tools in communications technology, such as Skype, Google+ Hangout, and WebEx, allow her to take her "survival job" one step further. "A few months ago I went out of the country to do a fencing retreat," she said. "I do a lot of different things as an actor and performer, and choreographing sword fights is one of them. So I was at a fencing school in France for two weeks, and I had a student who needed to see me. He was in DC, so we connected by Skype, and it worked out great. I can take my work with me wherever I go."

Because of online connectivity tools she hasn't had to miss an audition in three years. What's more, being able to tutor online has helped her with the ongoing struggle of maintaining her passion for acting and not taking the comfortable route. "I work very hard at *not* becoming a full-time professional tutor," she said. "When tutoring starts to take over my life, I will actually say no to certain tutoring assignments. In fact that's the biggest thing you have to watch for with the 'survival job.' I have had several actor friends in LA who had wonderful day jobs where their bosses let them take off if they had auditions. But eventually the day job became the thing they were thinking about all the time. And, especially in LA, you really start to rely on that financial security. Then you get the car and the clothes, and the next thing you know, you're not an actor anymore."

It's not a perfect life, but Nafeesa has forged a workable balance between her passion and her livelihood when many of her contemporaries have given up the dream. She would be perfectly content to continue building this kind of life: tutoring kids for the SAT, sometimes in person and sometimes online, pursuing acting jobs in Los Angeles, and building her children's theater company in Washington, DC. "I do relish my freedom and my flexibility. I'm very grateful for those things. I don't always have financial freedom, but just having those choices of what to do with my day, what to do with my life, and do something that creates meaning for me is a real gift and a real joy."[8]

THE END: BACK TO THE BEGINNING

In the beginning there was work, that fundamental, nonnegotiable condition of our existence. And no matter the advances in technology—from better technology to hunt that wily woolly

mammoth to better technology to assemble bits and bytes—
work will always be with us. In fact, if we've demonstrated
nothing else in this book, we hope we've established this one
simple fact of the Naked Economy: when we strip work bare
of all trappings, tools, and technologies that we've clothed it in
over the millennia, we're left with just . . . us.

That's right, just us, all seven billion of us, who wake up every morning and ask the age-old question: How are we going to
make a living today? Any economy, naked or otherwise, is designed to assemble our various talents, ideas, and energies in
an effort to answer this simple question. The real power of the
Naked Economy is a renewed understanding that cube farms,
smart phones, 401(k) plans, and long commutes don't make
the economy go. People do. Putting people—their productivity, their passions, their families, and their happiness—back at
the center of our thinking about work is the key to building a
vibrant, sane, sustainable, and profitable future.

Indeed, with the rise of the Naked Economy, we stand on
the cusp of a once-in-a-century opportunity: the possibility
of making a living while also making a life. Perhaps the great
Richard Florida put it best: "Today, for perhaps the first time in
human history, we have the opportunity to align economic and
human development."[9]

We'll close with the same question we opened with: Are you
ready for the Naked Economy? Great, so are we. We hope that,
after you've read this book, you're a bit more inspired too. So
let's get going. We have work to do, passions to follow, value to
create, impacts to make, and legacies to leave. As always, clothing is optional.

ACKNOWLEDGMENTS

In this book we describe a new project-based economy in which teams of specialists and generalists swarm around a particular task together, share their ideas and expertise, and (it is hoped) create something valuable and innovative. Indeed, that's a lot like how we wrote this book. We hope it stands as a small example of the power of this new economy. We have been incredibly lucky to work with a team of thinkers, researchers, coworkers, and cheerleaders who made every word possible by working with us and sticking with it much longer than any of us anticipated.

First and foremost, our sincerest thanks to Wallace Baine, a Santa Cruz–based writer who took a good story and helped us develop a narrative that would not have been possible without his considerable talents and patience.

At NextSpace we would like to thank our cofounder, Caleb Baskin. He was the first person to believe in our ideas, and that belief has never wavered. We're also deeply grateful to our founding board members—Kurt Grutzmacher, Jim Weisenstein, and Khristina Horn—and all the investors who believed in us when we had this kooky idea that people needed a different place and a different way to work. Thanks also to Chelsea Rustrum, Margaret Rosas, and Sol Lipman, who kicked us in the butt—literally and figuratively—and encouraged us to make it happen.

We had a team of student researchers from the University of California's Santa Cruz campus who worked many caffeinated nights finding us just the right fact or person for our story. Chief among them was Jocelyn Robinson, who saw the project through from beginning to end. Other researchers were Joey Klein, Max Casillas, Nora Lewis, Katie Holms, Grant Glander, and many others who jumped in between classes and during beer runs.

Anyone with a good story should contact James Levine of Levine Greenberg Literary Agency, the agent who made this happen. And when he finds you a publisher, we hope you will be lucky enough to have an editor like Laurie Harting at Palgrave, who will be there to remind you to find your voice and that you are not as funny as you think you are before handing you off to the meticulous and talented production editor Donna Cherry and copy editor Polly Kummel.

Speaking of people who reminded us that we are not that funny, thank you to Casey Protti, Sandy Skees, and Greg Neuner for reading and commenting on the manuscript. We are solely responsible for all errors and omissions, but there are a lot less of them because of you. A very special thanks to Jill Murphy, who, apropos of the technology that fuels the Naked Economy, may be the first person to critique a manuscript entirely by text message. Jill's patient reading of various drafts, her spot-on suggestions, and her gentle insistence that certain parts really needed work made this book much better. More important, Jill was the first person to tell us that our ideas and our writing actually had merit. That kind of validation was sweet, soothing balm for our fragile egos.

Thank you to all the members of NextSpace and to all the people in the emerging coworking industry around the world. Believe it: You really are changing the world for the better. That's a daunting task and you approach that task with leadership, passion, grace, and a ton of hard work. No one personifies those attributes more than Iris Kavanagh and Rebecca Brian. You guys rock.

Finally, we want to thank our children. We promise never to make you read this book. But we also promise to keep striving to create a new economy that allows you to work at your creative, innovative, and productive best.

NOTES

INTRODUCTION: THE NAKED ECONOMY

1. Daniel H. Pink, *Free Agent Nation: The Future of Working for Yourself* (New York: Business Plus, 2002); Richard Florida, *The Rise of the Creative Class: And How It's Transforming Work, Leisure, Community and Everyday Life* (New York: Basic Books, 2012).
2. Sara Horowitz, *The Freelancer's Bible: Everything You Need to Know to Have the Career of Your Dreams—On Your Terms* (New York: Workman, 2012).

CHAPTER 1: WE ARE ALL SELF-EMPLOYED

1. Shane Pearlman, interview by authors, July, 14, 2012, Capitola, California.
2. Dalton Conley, *Elsewhere, U.S.A: How We Got from the Company Man, Family Dinners, and the Affluent Society to the Home Office, BlackBerry Moms, and Economic Anxiety* (New York: Pantheon Books, 2009).
3. Alan Blinder, "How Many U.S. Jobs Might Be Offshoreable?" Center for European Policy Studies: Working Paper 10.2. 41-78 (March 2007).
4. Chris Guillebeau, *The $100 Startup: Reinvent the Way You Make a Living, Do What You Love, and Create a New Future* (New York: Crown Business, 2012).
5. Chris Guillebeau, *$100 Start Up;* What's Next Lectures, NextSpace, Santa Cruz, May 26, 2012.
6. Sheryl Jean, "Entrepreneurship Gives Dallas-Area Teens a Head Start," *Dallas Morning News,* May 16, 2011; Alexandra Cheney, "30 Under 30," *Inc.* Web, January 26, 2012.
7. Ulrica von Thiele Schwarz, "Employee Self-rated Productivity and Objective Organizational Production Levels," *Journal of Occupational and Environmental Medicine* 53.8. 838-844 (2011); Michelle Castillo, "Sitting too much may double your risk of dying, study shows," *CBS News,* March 27, 2012, http://www.cbsnews.com/8301-504763_162-57405178 -10391704/sitting-too-much-may-double-your-risk-of-dying-study- shows/; James A. Levine, "What are the risks of sitting too much?—Adult Health," Mayo Clinic, www.mayoclinic.com/health/sitting/AN02082 and www.cbsnews.com/8301-504763_162-57405178-10391704/sitting- too-much-may-double-your-risk-of-dying-study-shows/.

8. Stacy Crook and Michael Shirer, "Mobile Worker Population to Reach 1.3 Billion by 2015, According to IDC," press release, International Data Corporation, Framingham, Massachusetts, January 5, 2012.
9. "New Survey Reveals Overwhelming Demand for Virtual Collaboration," press release, Wrike, San Jose, California, March 21, 2012.
10. Renata de LaRocque, interview with authors, October 21, 2012, Santa Cruz, California.

CHAPTER 2: FROM HUNTER-GATHERERS TO TPS REPORTS

1. Marshall Sahlins, *Stone Age Economics* (Hawthorne, NY: Aldine de Gruyter, 1972).
2. Matt Ridley, "Human Evolution Isn't What It Used to Be," *Wall Street Journal,* May 24, 2012, http://online.wsj.com/article/SB1000142405270 2303610504577418511907146478.html.
3. Thomas Jefferson, *The Papers of Thomas Jefferson: 1787–1788* (Princeton, NJ: Princeton University Press, 1955), 12.
4. Jay P. Wilkinson, "The Impacts of Industrial Paternalism: A Study of the National Cash Register Company," *Middle States Geographer* 28 (1995): 87.
5. N. Gregory Mankiw, *Macroeconomics* (New York: Worth, 2010).
6. Daniel Gross, "Goodbye, Pension. Goodbye, Health Insurance. Goodbye, Vacations," *Slate,* September 23, 2004, http://www.slate.com/articles /business/moneybox/2004/09/goodbye_pension_goodbye_health_ins urance_goodbye_vacations.html.
7. Ibid.
8. C. Wright Mills, *The Power Elite* (New York, New York: Oxford University Press, 1956), 6.

CHAPTER 3: DUDE, WHERE'S MY PENSION?

1. Ben Gran, telephone interview with authors, June 29, 2012.
2. Thomas Hobbes. *The Leviathan* (Cambridge University Press, 1904), 84.
3. Gran, interview.
4. *David Arp et al. v. Whirlpool Corporation,* Case No. 3:12 CV 770 (July 10, 2012).
5. Gran, interview.
6. U.S. Department of Labor, "Quick Stats on Women Workers, 2010." *Women's Bureau—Data and Statistics,* 2010, http://www.dol.gov/wb /factsheets/QS-womenwork2010.htm#.UMYZRORZWRg%5D%5D.
7. US Bureau of Labor Statistics, *Current Population Survey, Employment Characteristics of Families,* "Table 6: Employment Status of Mothers with Own Children under 3 Years Old by Single Year of Age of Youngest Child and Marital Status," 2009-2010 Annual Averages (2011).
8. Hanna Rosin, *The End of Men: And the Rise of Women* (New York: Riverhead, 2012).
9. Jessica Arons, Heather Boushey, and Lauren Smith, "Why Aren't We There Yet?" Fact sheet, Center for American Progress, April 27, 2009, http:// www.americanprogress.org/issues/women/news/2009/04/27/5880 /why-arent-we-there-yet/.

10. Executive Office of the President, Council of Economics Advisers, *Work-Life Balance and the Economics of Workplace Flexibility: Executive Summary* March 2010, http://www.whitehouse.gov/files/documents/100331-cea-economics-workplace-flexibility.pdf.

11. US Bureau of Labor Statistics, Current Population Survey, "Table 5: Employment Status of the Population by Sex, Marital Status, and Presence and Age of Own Children under 18, 2010-2011 Annual Averages," (2012).

12. Ibid.

13. Sandy Skees, interview with authors, October 14, 2012, Santa Cruz, California.

14. Ibid.

15. Howard S. Friedman and Leslie R. Martin, *The Longevity Project: Surprising Discoveries for Health and Long Life from the Landmark Eight-Decade Study* (New York, Hudson Street Press, 2012).

16. Emily Yoffe, "What's the Secret to Living Longer and Being Healthier? Keep Doing Useful Work," *Slate*, March 10, 2011, http://www.slate.com/articles/life/silver_lining/2011/03/dont_stop_working.single.html. Ibid.

17. US Bureau of Labor Statistics, "Older Workers: Are There More Older People in the Workplace?" July 2008, http://www.bls.gov/spotlight/2008/older_workers/.

18. Arthur Delaney, "Baby Boomer Poll by AARP Finds Half Don't Expect to Retire," *Huffington Post*, August 8, 2012.

19. Ruth Helman, Craig Copeland, and Jack VanDerhei, "Preparing for Retirement In America: 2012 RCS Fact Sheet #3," Employee Benefit Research Institute, (2012).

20. Ibid.

21. Barbara Butrica, Howard Iams, Karen Smith, and Eric Toder, "The Disappearing Defined Benefit Pension and Its Potential Impact on the Retirement Incomes of Baby Boomers," *Social Security Bulletin* 69, no. 3 (2009): 1–27.

22. Peter Longman, "Hole in the Bucket," *Washington Monthly*, July/August 2012, 1.

23. Michelle Conlin, Moira Herbst, and Peter Coy, "The Disposable Worker," *Businessweek*, January 7, 2010.

24. Steven Wishnia, "A Nation of Temps," *Salon*, August 22, 2012.

25. Conlin, Herbst, and Coy, "Disposable Worker."

26. Linton Weeks, "A Temporary Solution for a New American Worker," NPR.org, December 14, 2010.

27. Steven Greenhouse, "A Part Time Life, as Hours Shrink and Shift," *New York Times*, October 28, 2012, A1.

28. Chrystia Freeland, *Plutocrats: The Rise of the New Global Super-Rich and the Fall of Everyone Else* (New York: Penguin Books, 2012), 27.

29. Charles Duhigg and Keith Bradsher, "The iEconomy: How the U.S. Lost Out on iPhone Work," *New York Times*, January 21, 2012.

30. US Bureau of Labor Statistics, *Union Membership Annual Report, 2011*, January 30, 2012. http://www.bls.gov/opub/ted/2012/ted_20120130.htm.

31. James T. Bennett, and Bruce E. Kaufman. *The Future of Private Sector Unionism In the United States* (Armonk, NY: M.E. Sharpe, 2002).

32. Joseph Stiglitz, *The Price of Inequality: How Today's Divided Society Endangers Our Future* (New York: W. W. Norton, 2012), 3.

33. Jim Clifton, *The Coming Jobs War* (New York: Gallup Press, 2011).

34. Stiglitz, *Price of Inequality.*

35. Thomas Kochan and Beth Shulman, "The Agenda for Shared Prosperity," EconomicPolicy Institute, February 22, 2012. http://www.epi.org/news/the-agenda-for-shared-prosperity/.

36. Richard Florida, *The Rise of the Creative Class and How It's Transforming Work, Leisure, Community and Everyday Life* (New York: Basic Books, 2012), 91.

37. Ibid., 135.

38. Skees, interview.

39. Gran, interview.

40. Jeanne Meister and Karie Willyerd, *The 2020 Workplace: How Innovative Companies Attract, Develop, and Keep Tomorrow's Employees Today* (New York: Harper Business, 2010).

41. Sylvia Ann Hewlett, Laura Sherbin, and Karen Sumberg, "How Gen Y and Boomers Will Reshape Your Agenda," *Harvard Business Review,* July 2009, 2-3.

42. Gran, interview.

CHAPTER 4: IF YOU ARE SPECIAL AND YOU KNOW IT . . . GET NAKED

1. Wallace J. Nichols, interview with authors, September 20, 2012, Santa Cruz, CA.

2. Jody Greenstone Miller and Matt Miller, "The Rise of the Supertemp," *Harvard Business Review,* May 2012, 50–62.

3. Thomas W. Malone, Robert J. Laubacher, and Tammy Johns, "The Age of Hyperspecialization," *Harvard Business Review,* July–August 2011, 58, 65, 61.

4. Ibid.

5. Ibid.

6. Jody Greenstone Miller, telephone interview with authors, September 24, 2012, Los Angeles, CA.

7. Ibid.

8. Julie Gupta, telephone interview with authors, September 28, 2012, Washington DC.

9. Ibid.

10. Miller, interview.

11. "Mechanical Turk Case Study: CastingWords," Amazon Web Services, n.d., http://aws.amazon.com/solutions/case-studies/castingwords-interview/.

12. Miller, interview.

13. Ibid.

14. Nichols, interview.

15. Ibid.

CHAPTER 5: THE GENERALLY BRIGHT FUTURE FOR SMART GENERALISTS

1. Liz Coleman, "Liz Coleman's Call to Reinvent Liberal Arts Education," TED: Ideas Worth Spreading, February 2009, http://www.ted.com/talks/liz_coleman_s_call_to_reinvent_liberal_arts_education.html.

2. E. D. Hirsch, Jr., *Cultural Literacy* (New York: Vintage 1987), 4.
3. Coleman, "Liz Coleman's Call."
4. Ibid.
5. Liz Coleman, "Bringing Back the Generalist," DGREE Conference, 2010, http://vimeo.com/9502076.
6. Ibid.
7. Paul Sullivan, "Scrutinizing the Elite Whether They Like it or Not," *New York Times,* October 15, 2010.
8. David Bollier, *The Future of Work: What It Means for Individuals, Businesses, Markets and Governments* (Aspen, CO: Aspen Institute, 2010), 8.
9. Dalton Conley, *Elsewhere, U.S.A: How We Got from the Company Man, Family Dinners, and the Affluent to the Home Office, BlackBerry Moms, and Economic Anxiety* (New York: Vintage Books, 2010), 59.
10. Richard Arum, Josipa Roksa, and Esther Cho, *Improving Undergraduate Learning: Findings and Policy Recommendations from the SSRC-CLA Longitudinal Project,* 11 (New York: Social Science Research Counsel, 2011).
11. Keith Christian, phone interview with authors, June 22, 2012, Los Angeles, CA.
12. Ibid.
13. Kellie Martin phone interview with authors, June 18, 2012, Los Angeles, CA.
14. Liz Coleman, DGREE Conference 2010.
15. Walter Isaacson, "Inventing the Future," *New York Times,* April 6, 2012.
16. Dan H. Pink, *A Whole New Mind: Why Right-Brainers Will Rule the Future* (New York: Riverhead Trade, 2006), 1.

CHAPTER 6: BARELY CORPORATE

1. Daniel H. Pink, *Free Agent Nation: The Future of Working for Yourself* (New York: Warner, 2001).
2. Amy C. Edmondson, "Teamwork on the Fly," *Harvard Business Review,* April 2012.
3. Bridgette Meinhold, "The Watercube Wins Australia's Highest Architecture Aware," *Inhabitat,* November 6, 2008, http://inhabitat.com/the-watercube-wins-australias-highest-architecture-award/.
4. Ibid.
5. Ella Miron-Spektor, Miriam Erez, and Eitan Naveh, "To Drive Creativity, Add Some Conformity," *Harvard Business Review,* March 2012.
6. InnoCentive, http://www.innocentive.com/.
7. Alissa Walker, "BP to InnoCentive: Sorry, We Don't Want Your 908 Ideas for Saving the Gulf," *Fast Company,* June 22, 2010, http://www.fastcompany.com/1663156/bp-innocentive-sorry-we-dont-want-your-908-ideas-saving-gulf.
8. InnoCentive, http://www.innocentive.com/.
9. David Bollier, "The Future of Work: What It Means for Individuals, Businesses, Markets and Governments," Aspen Institute, 2010, 10.
10. Jonathan Zittrain, "Work the New Digital Sweatshops," *Newsweek,* December 7, 2009.
11. This quote and others used in this section comes from the Freelancers Union website, http://www.freelancersunion.org/.
12. Kara Swisher, "Physically Together," AllThingsD.com, February 22, 2013, http://allthingsd.com/20130222/physically-together-heres-the

-internal-yahoo-no-work-from-home-memo-which-extends-beyond
-remote-workers/.
13. Matthew Mullenweg, interview with Ryan Coonerty, September 19, 2012, Monterey, CA.
14. Automattic, http://automattic.com/.
15. Mullenweg, interview.
16. Ibid.
17. Jeanne C. Meister and Karie Willyerd, *The 2020 Workplace: How Innovative Companies Attract, Develop, and Keep Tomorrow's Employees Today* (New York: Harper Business, 2010).

CHAPTER 7: PEOPLE

1. "Born on a Bike Seat," NBBFILMS, https://www.youtube.com/watch?v=mQlfuAYMNrc.
2. Gordy Mergoz, "The 30 Best Places to Work," Outside Online, http://www.outsideonline.com/outdoor-adventure/best-jobs/The-30-Best-Places-to-Work-of-2012.html.
3. "New Belgium Brewing," report, New Belgium Brewing Company, http://www.winningworkplaces.org/library/success/NewBelgium.pdf.
4. Ibid.
5. Bryan Simpson, phone interview with authors, January 28, 2013, Fort Collins, CO.
6. Devin Leonard, "New Belgium and the Battle of the Microbrews," *Bloomberg Businessweek*, December 1, 2011, http://www.businessweek.com/magazine/new-belgium-and-the-battle-of-the-microbrews-12012011.html.
7. Philip Rosedale, interview with authors, September 18, 2012, San Francisco, CA.
8. Ibid.
9. Ibid.
10. Ibid.
11. A. D. Amar, Carsten Hentrich, and Vlatka Hlupic, "To Be a Better Leader, Give Up Authority," *Harvard Business Review*, December 2009.
12. Rosedale, interview.

CHAPTER 8: PLACE

1. Mark Greiner, telephone interview with Jeremy Neuner, July 24, 2012.
2. Emergent Research and Intuit, *Intuit 2020 Report: Twenty Trends That Will Shape the Next Decade* (Mountain View, CA: Intuit, October 2010), http://http-download.intuit.com/http.intuit/CMO/intuit/futureofsmallbusiness/intuit_2020_report.pdf.
3. Robert D. Putnam, *Bowling Alone: The Collapse and Revival of American Community* (New York: Simon and Schuster, 2000).
4. Stephen Marche, "Is Facebook Making Us Lonely?" *Atlantic*, May 2012, http://www.theatlantic.com/magazine/archive/2012/05/is-facebook-making-us-lonely/308930/.
5. "Second Annual Global Coworking Survey," (Berlin) *Deskmag*, 2012, http://www.deskmag.com/en/the-birth-of-coworking-spaces-global-survey-176.

6. Ed Nolan, interview with Jeremy Neuner, September 20, 2012, Baltimore, MD.
7. Fred Bernstein, "Work in Context," *Dialogue* 18, July 9, 2010, 2, http://m.gensler.com/uploads/documents/D18%20_07_09_2010.pdf.
8. Jay Baughman, interview with Jeremy Neuner, September 21, 2012, Baltimore, MD.
9. Kevin Kuske, interview with Jeremy Neuner, September 20, 2012, Baltimore, MD.

CHAPTER 9: POLICY

1. Catherine Rampell, "When Job-Creation Engines Stop at Just One," *New York Times,* October 4, 2012.
2. E. J. Reedy and Robert E. Litan, *Starting Smaller; Staying Smaller: America's Slow Leak in Job Creation,* Research Series: Firm Formation and Economic Growth (Kansas City, MO: Ewing Marion Kauffman Foundation, July 2011).
3. Sara Horowitz, Hollis Calhoun, Althea Erickson, and Gabrielle Wuolo, "America's Uncounted Independent Workforce," Freelancers Union, 2011, 4, www.FreelancersUnion.org.
4. Sean McMurray, telephone interview with Jeremy Neuner, October 8, 2012.
5. Robert W. Fairlie, Kanika Kapur, and Susan M. Gates, "Is Employer-Based Health Insurance a Barrier to Entrepreneurship?" Working paper of the Kauffman-Rand Institute for Entrepreneurship Public Policy, Santa Monica, CA, September 2010, ix.
6. Emergent Research and Intuit, *Intuit 2020 Report: Twenty Trends That Will Shape the Next Decade* (Mountain View, CA: Intuit, October 2010), http://http-download.intuit.com/http.intuit/CMO/intuit/futureofsmallbusiness/intuit_2020_report.pdf.
7. Shane Pearlman, interview with authors, July 14, 2012, Capitola, CA.
8. Sara Horowitz et al., "Americas Uncounted Independent Workforce," www.FreelancersUnion.org.
9. United Nations, Department of Economic and Social Affairs, "World Urbanization Prospects 2011." April 5, 2012.
10. For more information about the TED Prize, see http://www.thecity2.org/.
11. Richard Florida, *The Rise of the Creative Class,* 3rd ed. (New York: Basic Books, 2012), 259.
12. Ibid., 293.
13. Jim Clifton, *The Coming Jobs War* (New York: Gallup Press, 2011), 12.
14. Edward Glaeser and William Kerr, "The Secret to Job Growth: Think Small," *Harvard Business Review,* July 2010, 4.
15. Richard Adler, *The Dilbert Paradox* (Washington DC: Aspen Institute, 2011), 30.
16. "Benefits of Days at Work," Humane Society, http://www.humanesociety.org/news/press_releases/2010/08/benefits_of_dogs_at_work_081710.html
17. Diana Rothschild, interview by Jeremy Neuner, January 22, 2013, San Francisco, CA
18. "100 Best Companies to Work For," CNN Money, http://money.cnn.com/magazines/fortune/best-companies/2012/benefits/child_care.html.

19. Reid Hoffman and Ben Casnocha, *The Start-up of You: Adapt to the Future, Invest in Yourself, and Transform Your Career* (New York: Crown Business, 2012), 8.
20. Jeffrey Gangemi, "Young, Fearless and Smart," *Businessweek,* October 30, 2006.
21. Shaila Dewan, "To Stay Relevant in a Career, Workers Train Nonstop," *New York Times,* September 21, 2012.
22. Hoffman and Casnocha, *Start-up of You.*
23. Andy Grove, "How America Can Create Jobs," *Bloomberg Businessweek,* July 1, 2010.

CHAPTER 10: WHAT TO EXPECT WHEN YOU'RE
EXPECTING THE NAKED ECONOMY

1. Heather Stephenson, telephone interview with Ryan Coonerty, September 14, 2012.
2. Danielle Sacks, "The Sharing Economy," *Fast Company,* April 18, 2011, http://www.fastcompany.com/1747551/sharing-economy.
3. Zach Hochstadt, telephone interview with Ryan Coonerty, September 6, 2012.
4. Alina Tugend, "The Workplace Benefits of Being Out of Touch," *New York Times,* July 13, 2012, http://www.nytimes.com/2012/07/14/your -money/companies-see-benefit-of-time-away-from-mobile-devices .html.
5. Donnie Fowler, telephone interview with Ryan Coonerty, August 28, 2012.
6. Spencer Lindsay, interview with Jeremy Neuner, September 22, 2012, Santa Cruz, CA.
7. Tess Finnegan, telephone interview with Jeremy Neuner, September 29, 2012.
8. Nafeesa Monroe, telephone interview with Ryan Coonerty, September 12, 2012.
9. Richard Florida, *The Creative Compact: An Economic and Social Agenda for the Creative Age,* www.creativeclass.com/rfcgdb/articles/The _Creative_Compact.pdf.

SOME RECOMMENDED READING

BIG TRENDS

Anderson, Chris. *Makers: The New Industrial Revolution*. New York: Crown Business, 2012.

Bollier, David. *The Future of Work: What It Means for Individuals, Businesses, Markets and Governments*. Aspen Institute, 2010.

Conley, Dalton. *Elsewhere, U.S.A: How We Got from the Company Man, Family Dinners, and the Affluent Society to the Home Office, BlackBerry Moms, and Economic Anxiety*. New York: Pantheon Books, 2010.

Cuilla, Joanne. *The Working Life: The Promise and Betrayal of Modern Work*. New York: Crown Business, 2001.

Florida, Richard. *The Great Reset: How New Ways of Living and Working Drive Post-Crash Prosperity*. New York: Harper Business, 2010.

———. *The Rise of The Creative Class: And How It's Transforming Work, Leisure, Community and Everyday Life*. New York: Basic Books, 2012.

Freeland, Chrystia. *Plutocrats: The Rise of the New Global Super-Rich and the Fall of Everyone Else*. London: Penguin, 2012.

Johnson, Steven. *Where Good Ideas Come From: The Natural History of Innovation*. New York: Riverhead Hardcover, 2010.

Pink, Daniel H. *A Whole New Mind: Why Right-Brainers Will Rule the Future*. New York: Penguin, 2005.

———. *Free Agent Nation: The Future of Working for Yourself*. New York: Business Plus, 2002.

Putnam, Robert D. *Bowling Alone: The Collapse and Revival of American Community*. New York: Touchstone, 2001.

Stiglitz, Joseph E. *The Price of Inequality: How Today's Divided Society Endangers Our Future*. New York: W. W. Norton, 2012.

Future of Talent Institute (futureoftalent.org)

Institute for the Future (iftf.org/home/)

Kauffman Foundation (www.kauffman.org)

NEW ORGANIZATIONS

Brafman, Ori and Rod A. Beckstrom. *The Starfish and the Spider: The Unstoppable Power of Leaderless Organizations*. New York: Portfolio Trade, 2008.

Edmondson, Amy C. *Teaming: How Organizations Learn, Innovate, Learn, and Compete in the Knowledge Economy.* San Francisco: Jossey-Bass, 2012.

Fried, Jason. *ReWork.* New York: Crown Business, 2010.

Godin, Seth. *Linchpin: Are You Indispensable?* New York: Portfolio Trade, 2011.

Howe, Jeff. *Crowdsourcing: Why the Power of the Crowd Is Driving the Future of Business.* New York: Crown Business, 2008.

Malone, Michael. *The Future Arrived Yesterday: The Rise of the Protean Corporation and What It Means for You.* New York: Crown Business, 2009.

Meister, Jeanne C., and Karie Willyerd. *The 2020 Workplace: How Innovative Companies Attract, Develop, and Keep Tomorrow's Employees Today.* New York: Harper Business, 2010.

Pink, Daniel H. *Drive: The Surprising Truth About What Motivates Us.* New York: Riverhead Trade, 2011.

COWORKING

Coworking, http://coworking.com/

Nextspace, http://nextspace.us/

GOING NAKED

Ferriss, Timothy. *The 4-Hour Workweek: Escape 9–5, Live Anywhere, and Join the New Rich.* New York: Ebury, 2011.

Guillebeau, Chris. *The $100 Startup: Reinvent the Way You Make a Living, Do What You Love, and Create a New Future.* New York: Crown Business, 2012.

Hoffman, Reid, and Ben Casnocha. *The Start-up of You: Adapt to the Future, Invest in Yourself, and Transform Your Career.* New York: Crown Business, 2012.

Horowitz, Sara, and Toni Sciarra Poynter. *The Freelancer's Bible: Everything You Need to Know to Have the Career of Your Dreams—On Your Terms.* New York: Workman, 2012.

Muller, Thor, and Lane Becker. *Get Lucky: How to Put Planned Serendipity to Work for You and Your Business.* San Francisco: Jossey-Bass, 2012.

Seelig, Tina. *What I Wish I Knew When I was 20.* New York: HarperOne, 2009.

Slim, Pamela. *Escape from Cubicle Nation: From Corporate Prisoner to Thriving Entrepreneur.* New York: Portfolio Hardcover, 2009.

Vaynerchuk, Gary. *Crush It! Why NOW Is the Time to Cash in on Your Passion.* New York: Harper Studio, 2009.

INDEX